Getting More Out of Progress Monitoring

Forms and Ideas to Help You Improve the Reading Skills of

Lower Elementary Students

Curt Foust

"For Reid and Quinn-My two favorite readers"

Proofreading by Brooke Hall
Formatting by Porsché Steele
Additional editing by Britney Moritz
Cover design by Danijela Mijailovic

Text copyright © 2019
Published by KDP

ISBN-10: 1701143852
ISBN-13: 978-1701143852

www.foustreading.simplesite.com verified as of December 2019

Table of Contents

Chapter One

Introduction

(or "Why am I writing this book?")

Why am I writing this?

First and foremost, teaching reading is a passion of mine. I especially love teaching younger elementary students. This is a very exciting time in their lives as they start to explore language. There is just something amazing about a child learning to read. From the beginning stages of learning about sounds to the later stages of reading whole words and putting sentences together, it is awesome to see these processes click in their brains.

There are several phases and stages of reading that the young reader must pass through to become a fluent and proficient reader. During these stages, there are many areas of reading that need to be addressed. Three big areas are decoding (phonics), fluency, and comprehension. When teaching reading, we need to keep a focus on all these areas and make sure the students are adequately progressing. Losing focus on one area can be detrimental to other areas. Another thing that may happen is thinking a child is sufficient in one area and moving on to the next area before it is time. These are all common and understandable mistakes to make. I certainly have made these mistakes in the past. However, I have learned to be aware of these mistakes and have developed techniques to help avoid making these mistakes in the future.

Over my eighteen years of teaching reading to young students, I have developed several charts and graphs to help me **progress monitor** the students. By **progress monitoring**, I mean keeping track of the student's progress (data) by noting and comparing assessment scores. This could be one-minute reading assessments, test scores like DIBELS or STAR, or their grades on classroom assignments. Using a combination of many different sources would be ideal. Progress monitoring must also be done in a consistent and regular way. We must be able to take our progress monitoring results and use them effectively. Our data will not help us unless we find a way to make it accessible and understandable.

My hope is to present you with something you can use to keep all your important scores and data in one place, a place that you can easily revisit. This data must also be presented in a way that is easy to read. This will benefit you immensely in developing effective interventions for your students. At the same time, you want something you can share with parents. Therefore, you want something parents will be able to easily understand. All the forms in this book have been created in Google Docs and can easily be changed to fit your needs.

What is RTI?

Before we start, we need to understand what RTI is. This term will be used throughout the book. What follows is a simplified definition. RTI stands for **Response to Intervention**. We use this process to identify what kinds of interventions should be used for our students. There are three levels or groupings of students in the RTI process. **Tier I** includes all the students in a particular class. This is the instruction that everyone receives. Please see the figure 1.1 after this section.

Tier II is a smaller group of students (within the bigger group) who are identified as needing extra help. The students are initially selected for this group by analyzing data. Those who are not reaching the level of success expected at that point in the year are considered Tier II. This group is usually given extra intervention as a group in addition to normal instruction. This could include pull-out services such as Title One reading classes.

Tier III would include students from the Tier II group who are not progressing with the extra interventions given. Tier III groups are usually given one on one instruction at least three times a week. Intervention time should be around 30 minutes a session. This book will deal with getting the most out of this extra reading intervention time via graphs geared toward tracking the progress of our students. Doing this allows us to maximize the time we have and make sure we make the most out of our time.

The school I currently teach at embraced the RTI process over 10 years ago. When we first started, we all felt overwhelmed in learning this new process. There is a lot to understand. For example, tracking the results of each student can be daunting. However, every year the process became easier to understand and implement. Finding a good way to track data is a key part to the RTI process. Once you find something that works for you, the RTI process will become more and more effective. Hopefully, what I have created and used over the years will help you direct the focus of your interventions. Please understand right from the beginning that you can modify my forms to suit your needs. Everything I present to you here is not set in stone. Every form used in this book is available at www.foustreading.simplesite.com. You will also be supplied with several blank forms in the back of this book that you can pick and choose from.

Figure 1.1

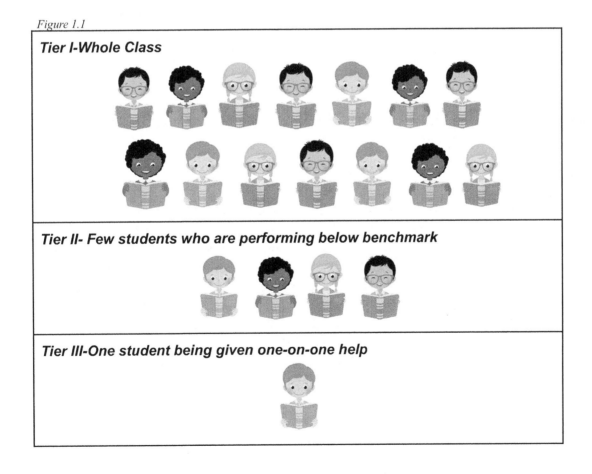

4

Overview: Making the Most of the Time We Have

Obviously, reading is an incredibly important skill. Therefore, how reading is taught is vital. Time, of course, can be and often is very limited. We must make the most out of the time we have. This book deals with techniques and tools I have developed over time to assist me with this task. In order to accomplish these time-saving techniques, we must first identify areas of weakness. Data needs to be kept and analyzed. A teacher, especially one who focuses on struggling readers, must do their best to pinpoint the types of errors their students make.

A teacher must have a way to organize this data. I use various graphic organizers. I have developed these graphic organizers over time with constant revision. Over the course of the last 15 years, I have made many adjustments to help make things easier to read. Also, I only want to put in the data that I feel is most useful. These organizers and charts are used to complement the RTI process by organizing the data into ways we can more easily analyze. By this, I simply mean we need to narrow our focus on understanding whether the data we have supports if a student is improving or not. Careful analysis must be used to choose the right intervention activities.

My hope is that after using and applying these methods and forms, you will be a stronger teacher in certain areas. **One**: You will be able to pick your lesson objectives and plan your lessons much more effectively. **Two**: You will increase your ability to pick out areas of concern just by listening to a student read. This may sound like a hard feat to accomplish, but knowing what to look for will help. This kind of information is exactly what we are keeping track of and organizing. **Three**: You will be more prepared and confident when meeting with parents. Parents are a huge part of the RTI process. You must utilize ways to bring them into the process and allow them to play a role in it **Four**: I want you to discover more ways to motivate your students. You can use some of these materials to motivate the students themselves and not just for the benefit of teachers and parents.

These steps are by no means all that I hope you can accomplish with this book; they are the areas I feel I have seen the most improvements in.

What is the focus of this book?

The main focus of this book is to introduce you to some teaching resources I have used over the years. I will share different methods I use when I progress monitor my own students. Remember that progress monitoring simply means regularly using assessments to check student progress. I use a variety of graphs, charts, and tables. Each one of these allows me to determine what I need to focus on when I plan my instruction for my students. The tables that you will read about are made for first and second graders. However—and this is important—you can easily modify the charts to be used for other grades. The areas focused on are decoding (phonics), fluency, and comprehension. These are very important areas in the teaching of reading. I know it may seem I am oversimplifying some concepts in this book. However, I truly believe in what I do, and my goal is to present the material in an easy-to-understand way.

Another important focus is to help make communication with parents easier. Many of my parents over the years have stated that they appreciate having the tables to look at. I want to be able to show parents what I do and why I do it. This makes them more knowledgeable about what I'm teaching their children. It is important to me that they, as parents, know I have a reason for what I am doing. By giving them reasoning and direction, this makes the parent feel more involved and more empowered to help their child.

I want to be able to show specific areas of growth or lack of growth. My forms easily point out specific student reading improvement. I want to justify my lessons and interventions by using the forms as solid evidence of what is happening with a parent's child. My thoughts are that if the parents believe in what you are doing, they will be more willing to spend the extra time doing what you suggest at home. You want to make a point of this to assure the parents that their time is not wasted.

I have refined and revised these tables many times over the past several years. It is possible, and maybe even likely, that you'll have to make the appropriate changes that will benefit you. However, I really feel using my reports will help your students in the areas of decoding, fluency, and comprehension. As with anything new, it will seem overwhelming to get started. I strongly encourage you to just go at it one step at a time. I want to stress this very strongly. Once you start to see data accumulate week after week, you will see the value of these forms.

Please keep the following things in mind.

1. **I do not want this book to be overwhelming.** There is a lot of information and ideas presented in this book. I want you to find what works for you. The idea is to help you find better ways to keep track of your data. In turn, I hope this makes it easier for you to plan effective interventions that have a focus. That way you don't waste time with interventions you don't need. I typically find that I can complete the whole process (forms and administration) in about five minutes per student. A teacher's aid or volunteer could be properly trained to administer and complete these forms.

2. **Remember that you can adapt these forms.** You do not need to use these forms exactly as I have them in this book. There are many different modified forms at the end that you can copy or use. Also, templates of the forms are available at www.foustreading.simplesite.com. I use certain assessments that are common to my school, but you can use other assessments.

3. **You do not need to use these with every child.** These forms are best for the students who are struggling with their reading. These forms are very good for TIER II and TIER III students. See the following chapter for more information on the RTI process.

4. **The data doesn't have to be perfect.** As you will find out, I track many kinds of data. One particular kind is in the area of tracking types of mistakes. Sometimes you simply have to use your best judgement while tracking errors. This process will become easier over time. Some of the data tracked is objective, such as rating certain skills on a scale of 1 to 4. This is fine as long as you are consistent in how you assign a rating.

5. **You can either type these forms or handwrite them.** While I prefer using the electronic versions because it is easy to read and share, the important thing is to have ways to keep and track your data.

6. **It's not just about data tracking.** Obviously data collecting is a huge part of this method, but it is not the only part. Using the forms over time will increase your ability to listen to a student and instantly pick out things that need improvement.

7. **This method can be used in most elementary grade levels.** Even though I will show examples from first and second grade, other grades can also benefit. I use first and second grade as examples because those grades are the ones that I have the most experience in. However, I have adapted these forms all the way up to fifth grade.

8. **I like to keep things simple.** This is especially true with interventions that I suggest. I am providing you with easy inexpensive examples that do not require too much extra effort.

Chapter Two

Terms to Know

(or "How can I get the most out of this book?")

The following chapter discusses different terms I use throughout the book. These definitions capture the meaning of the terms to help you best understand them in context. These descriptions are consistent throughout this book.

Decoding

Decoding is the ability to translate print into speech. There is the simpler task of providing the proper sound for the letter, then there is the more complex task of putting several letters together to make words. After this comes putting syllables together to make words. The hope is to perfect the more basic skill of sounding out letters, then move on to bigger words. Complicating this process are the words that do not follow the rules. Some students adapt very well to the exceptions to the rules while others do not. The forms I use are designed to pinpoint certain areas of decoding difficulty that can be focused on.

The goal, of course, is quick recognition of the syllables into whole words. It is also important the student does this with a smooth rhythm. Tracking data related to decoding includes types of errors and the frequency of these errors. The importance of knowing the type of error allows for us to adjust our interventions and focus on the areas the students need the most. Remember, we are trying to focus our intervention to make the most of the limited time that we have. For example, let's say we know a student made five mistakes during the reading of a one-minute passage. This information only shows us that there were five mistakes made and not the kinds of mistakes that were made. Knowing the type of error the student made helps us to focus on the more precise area that needs correcting. Possible types of errors include short vowel sounds, long vowel sounds, word beginnings, and word endings. Of course these are not the only types of errors. I will discuss others in upcoming chapters.

Fluency

Fluency is the ability to read orally with speed, accuracy, and proper expression (National Institute of Child Health and Human Development [NICHD], 2000). Another word used for reading with expression is prosody (Dowhower, 1991). Being fluent has also been described as the clear, easy written or spoken expression of ideas, freedom from word identification problems, and automaticity (McLaughlin & Fisher, 2005).

These two descriptions are not exactly the same but similar in noting that fluency is not just about reading quickly. This can be a difficult concept to get through to some students. Sometimes it is not easy to get them to realize that there is more beyond reading fast.

Why is reading fluency necessary? Reading fluently is necessary because fluent readers are able to minimize word-by-word reading, which can aid in comprehension (McLaughlin & Fisher). Comprehension, which will be described in more detail later, is the process by which meaning is constructed from words. Due to the amount of effort reading takes, a lack of fluency will usually have a negative effect on comprehension. The nice thing about fluency is that it allows itself to be tracked fairly easily. In this guide, I provide methods to present this information in a way that is easily viewed by parents and students alike.

You can keep track of fluency in different ways. However, there are a couple of different ways I utilize and find effective. The obvious one is words per minute. This is exactly what it sounds like—the total number of words the student can read in a minute. The passage should be from their grade level. The passage should also be from a similar reading level so you can more accurately compare scores to each other. More importantly, the reading of the passages must be checked on a regular basis. My preference is to administer these passages on a weekly basis.

Even though words per minute are a good indicator of fluency and easy to track, they are not the sole indicator we want to look at. A higher number of words is often a good indicator of fluency, but it can be misleading. I compare reading fluently to a reader sounding like they are taking part in a conversation with someone. This includes reading with expression (prosody). This is why I include a fluency rating that includes expression. This scale uses a rating of 1 to 4 and will be discussed in more detail later in this book. It is adapted from the National Assessment of Educational Progress (NAEP) Scale for Assessing Oral Reading Fluency.

Figure 2.1

Fluency

1. Slow, like a robot. Sounds out words.
2. OK, but still a little slow. May sound out a word or two.
3. Pretty good.
4. Perfect! Sounds like they are talking. Not too fast and not too slow. Reads with expression.

Sight Word Recognition

There are different ways to look at sight words. The way I determine a sight word is if it doesn't follow the normal decoding patterns that have already been taught. "The" would be a good example of this, along with words like "could" and "sight." Sight words are words that are encountered on a regular basis. These words may or may not sound out. As far as the irregular sounding out sight words, the student might try to sound out the word only to not have it make sense. In order to combat this, the goal is to have automatic recognition upon seeing the words. To illustrate this to my students, I snap my fingers when I explain automatic recognition. Quick recognition allows students to use more energy in decoding other words. We need quick recognition because having to stop and decode a word can really derail a student's ability to understand what they are reading.There are many ways to improve sight word recognition. The charts I use and will discuss help determine if sight words need to be the focus of additional intervention. The information on my forms will also help us choose what grade level of sight words to use. This is because there are many sets of sight words that have been arranged and grouped into different sets based on grade or reading level. One chart I use tracks the types of words missed. This is the One-Minute Reading Breakdown Chart (Form E) which is discussed in upcoming chapters. Doing this allows the teacher to take note of the types of words missed, including sight words.

Comprehension

What is comprehension? Comprehension is how something is understood or processed as it is being read. I think most would agree it is the ultimate goal of all reading interventions. There are various ways to estimate how well a student comprehends. These ways include retelling, questioning, clarifying unknown terms, and summarizing. The main goal with comprehension is to make a reader constantly think about what they are reading. It is important to realize that just because a student can read very fluently does not mean that they are able to process or make sense of what they read. I have seen many readers who are very fast readers but can't recall what they have read. If they can't, we need to determine why. Is it because they are reading too quickly or is there a real problem with processing? Reading without thinking about what is being read can be a hard habit to break. That is why we need to look beyond speed. Proper fluency is important, but it must lead to comprehension.

A benefit of using my tracking forms is that we can focus on what might be affecting comprehension. This includes ruling out certain issues. For example, let's say there are a lot of errors in a one-minute reading. This would be a good area to focus on. We would use the charts to determine whether the errors might be carelessness or if it is a decoding problem. Each issue requires a different approach. Another scenario might be that the student fluency charts look good, but we notice their retelling or testing is not showing the same proficiency. In this case we can implement comprehension graphic organizers and encourage the student to slow down and question what they are reading. At the end of this book are many organizers that can be used to aid comprehension.

Clarify

I decided to put clarify after decoding and comprehension for a reason. Clarify can mean using decoding to figure out an unknown word. In this case it is more about just knowing how the word sounds. However, clarify can also be what you do when you know what a word sounds like but you do not know what it means. A major part of this type of clarifying is using the words and sentences around the unknown word for clues to the meaning.

Progress Monitoring

As briefly mentioned earlier, progress monitoring is using data to keep a close eye on the gains a student is making (or not making) over time. We, of course, use this to monitor the progress (or lack of progress) a student is making in an area. A teacher needs to know what is working and what is not. That way we can add new interventions or drop ineffective ones. Progress monitoring does not need to be extremely detailed, but it does need to be consistent. This includes the difficulty of the material you are using in assessments. I suggest doing assessments once a week for students who are struggling. It also does not need to be time consuming. For students struggling in reading, a one-minute reading is a good way to do this. It does not take a lot of time to administer and many different trained people could administer it. You may think that you do not hear a lot in one minute. This may be true for some aspects, but it can show us a lot if you are consistent in their administration. After a few weeks, you will have an excellent set of data to look at.

Next, we will be looking at different forms that I use to keep track of the important data of each student I am working with. Over time, I have used five main forms and a form I share with parents that contains an overview of all my information. We will be going over one form per chapter. Within each chapter we will break apart each section and discuss in detail. After the chapter that introduces each form, I will use a real example from one of my students. My hope is that this will give you a better idea of what the forms are for and what you can gain from using these forms.

Chapter Three

Progress Monitoring Student Report (Form A)

(Or "How can I track many different types of data on one page?")

Let's take a look at a blank example of this form below.

Progress Monitoring Student Report (Form A)

DIBELS Results—January *(* means winter benchmark met)*

NWF (nonsense word fluency) 43/8-benchmark	ORF 23-benchmark	Retell n/a	Accuracy 78%	Composite 130-benchmark

DIBELS Results-September *(underlined if benchmark was met)*

LNF (letter naming fluency) No benchmark	PSF (phoneme segmentation fluency) 40-benchmark	NWF (nonsense word fluency) 27/1-benchmark	Composite 113

STAR and SEL *(Key: urg.=needs extra intervention, int.=needs intervention, OW-on watch [may need intervention], at=at or above benchmark)*

	STAR (SS, GE & IRL)	SEL	Baseline (total and alt. baseline)
#1			
#2			

Results of Progress Monitoring: *(underlined means first benchmark met, * Means second met, numbers in () indicate difference from last DIB)*

	LNF	PSF (40)	NWF (43/8)	ORF (23)	Retell (# and quality)	Accuracy
#1						
#2						
#3						
#4						
#5						
#6						
#7						
#8						
#9						
#10						

Next Benchmarks in April:

NWF	ORF (oral reading fluency)	Retell

AR:

Total Points	%	Level

Interventions Used:

*Key: **NWF**-reading made up words **ORF**-oral reading fluency (how many words read in a minute) **Composite**-a combination score of all the areas. **Retell # and quality**-How many words and how many details; 4 is best for quality. **STAR and SEL**-these are exams that test comprehension and other skills **GE**-grade equivalent, what level they tested **IRL**-instructional reading level, the level they should read at to improve (not too easy and not too hard)*

A part of a successful intervention program includes a way to effectively keep track of the data. It must be done in a way that is easy to complete and also easy to look at and understand. I use the Progress Monitoring Student Report (Form A) on the previous page. It will also be referred to as "Form A" for simplicity. I have successfully used this form for many years. I have been constantly adjusting it based on the needs of my students. At the back of this book are different blank versions that you can choose from that best meet your needs. You can also find templates online at www.foustreading.simplesite.com. You can also adjust these forms to meet your needs.

Form A allows me to keep a constant eye on the data while keeping all the important data on one page. It is the form I look at the most. Because of this, I want to make it very easy to read. Keeping it all on one page is important because that makes it easier to keep track of the data. This makes it easier to make a judgement of whether my interventions are working or not. We do not want to continue using an unsuccessful intervention. On this report, there are places to include test scores, weekly progress monitoring, interventions used, and any other information you feel is important.

The main idea is to have all your important information in one area to allow for analysis and presentation of the data. Form A is also useful for presenting information to the parents in an organized way. I have modified this chart many times over the years in order to make it more effective and easier to understand. The teacher could easily make any modification to fit their needs.

We are going to go over Form A one section at a time starting with the main assessment you will use throughout the year. In this case, we are using the DIBELS assessment.

Section One: Main Assessment Data

DIBELS Data (or other baseline data):

Figure 3.1

DIBELS Results-January *(* means winter benchmark met)*

NWF (nonsense word fluency)	ORF	Retell	Accuracy	Composite
43/8-benchmark	23-benchmark	n/a	78%	130-benchmark

DIBELS Results-September *(underlined if benchmark was met)*

LNF (letter naming fluency)	PSF (phoneme segmentation fluency)	NWF (nonsense word fluency)	Composite
No benchmark	40-benchmark	27/1-benchmark	113

Even though I use the DIBELS data as my baseline information, you could easily use other assessments. The key is to indicate which assessment you are using at the top of the chart. You can adjust the tables and change them to accommodate whatever assessment you are using. I would recommend keeping it simple; just put the most important scores on the chart. In the case of DIBELS, there are three administrations given. The latest is given at the top, in a bigger font than the others. I want it to stand out and be easy to read. In this example, I have two places for scores—the September and January administrations. That is because this is what the form looks like in the middle of the school year. You could easily add more. That is one of the benefits of using the electronic versions of these forms. I have also included blank forms in Appendix 1 that contain places for three administrations. The reason for having these assessment scores at the top is that it allows you to easily compare them to the progress monitoring results. Note that I have the recommended benchmark above their scores in the appropriate category. This is especially useful for the parents who may not necessarily know what a good or adequate score is. As we progress through the year, we will administer the DIBELS in the winter and the spring. I will add these scores as I obtain them. If I am using one of the electronic copies, I can add another section to it. However, I can also use forms that already have places for these administrations on them. This is ideal if you are handwriting the results in.

Key for Terms that Appear with the DIBELS Data

I will next go over some terms that appear in the section shown. These refer to the DIBELS assessment. All of these are from section one of Form A.

PSF *(Phoneme Segmentation Fluency)*. This is an assessment of how well the student does at breaking a word apart into its individual sounds. For example, if the student is given the word "cat," they would respond c-a-t. The ability to segment phonemes can be a good predictor of future decoding skills.

LNF *(Letter Naming Fluency)*. This is how many letters they were able to correctly say. This is only given in first grade during the fall administration; that is why it only shows up once on the chart. There is no benchmark for this area.

NWF *(Nonsense Word Fluency)*. The object of this section of the assessment is to see how skilled the student is at reading made-up words that sound out. The words are made up so that we know the students are not just memorizing words they already know. Memorization may make the child appear more adept at decoding than they really are. This score includes two numbers separated by a hyphen. The first number is the total number of sounds pronounced correctly. If the word was "nok," the student could say each sound with a pause and it would be correct. The second number means words that are said without a pause between each sound. In other words, the second number is the amount of words they read automatically without sounding out the individual sounds.

Section Two: Additional Assessment Results

Figure 3.2

	STAR (SS, GE & IRL)	SEL	Baseline (Total and Alt. Baseline)
#1			
#2			
#3			
#4			

This table displays other assessment data, besides the DIBELS assessment (figure 3.2). This can be any assessment you use to track student achievement. In the table below, I use the STAR Reading Assessment and the STAR Early Literacy Assessments by Renaissance Learning, the same company that produces Accelerated Reader. The final column is the baseline test provided by the reading series we use. This is given at the beginning of the year. Any reading assessments that you give can be listed here. As stated before, you can use any assessment here as long as you list the scores in order to make it easy to see if there is improvement.

Section Three: Weekly Progress Monitoring

Figure 3.3

Results of Progress Monitoring: *(underlined means first benchmark met, * Means second met, numbers in () indicate difference from last DIB)*

	LNF	PSF (40)	NWF (43/8)	ORF (23)	Retell (# and quality)	Accuracy
#1						
#2						
#3						
#4						
#5						
#6						
#7						
#8						
#9						
#10						
#11						
#12						
#13						
#14						
#15						

This section includes my weekly progress monitoring scores. I made the scores very easy to read and to compare with one another. If a benchmark is met, the score is underlined, or marked with a * or a ^, depending on the time of year it was administered. I use underlining if the first or fall benchmark is met. A * is used for the second or winter benchmark. A ^ is used for the third or spring benchmark. I wanted a way for the score to stand out if it is at benchmark. Just looking for these symbols will give us an idea if our intervention is working.

The headings of each column in this table are the same ones we see in section one. As stated before—LNF is letter naming fluency, PSF is phoneme segmentation, NWF is nonsense word fluency, and ORF is oral reading fluency. Retell involves two numbers. The first (#) is how many relevant words were told to me about the story and the second (quality) is how detailed the retell was on a scale of 1 to 4. To quickly review the retell scale, the first number is the total number of words recalled. This number gives us good information, but the second number is more important. The second number is the quality of the retell. A 1 is poor quality, a 2 is two details, a 3 is 3 details, and a 4 is 3 or more details told in a way that conveys the main idea.

Section Four: Benchmark for the Next DIBELS

Figure 3.4

Next Benchmarks in April:

NWF	ORF (oral reading fluency)	Retell

This section (figure 3.4) includes the benchmarks for the next administration of the DIBELS. This could be a different type of goal if you do not use DIBELS. It is useful to have it right there with my progress monitoring data for quick and easy comparison. Doing this also gives the parents an idea of what to expect in the near future. Also, allowing the student to know this benchmark can help the student be more focused on a goal. If the regular benchmark is an unreasonable goal, it is best to make a more reasonable goal for the student. Even if the new goal is below the next benchmark, we want it to be something attainable. It needs to be something that will take work and effort but not be unreachable.

Section Five: Additional Data

Figure 3.5

AR:

Total Points	%	Level

This section (figure 3.5) could include any other data you feel is important and necessary to include with the rest. For this example, scores from the Accelerated Reader program (AR) are included. I include these because we can get a good idea of a few different things from looking at this data. By taking a look at the total points we can see if the student is accumulating points. This might give an indication of their motivation. Looking at the percentage correct can give us a good idea if they are reading with accuracy. I have seen many students before with a substantial amount of points but also have a low percentage. This needs to be addressed but can easily be overlooked if we are just looking at points. I usually use 85% as the cutoff. Anything below this, I start to have concerns about why they are not doing as well as I would like. The student might be hurrying through just to get done. They might not be concerned about getting all the questions correct as long as they are passing. In cases like this, they need to be encouraged to slow down. They could read it out loud to you or someone else until you are convinced that they are reading it more thoroughly.

A more pressing concern might be that they are lacking the necessary strategies to comprehend or could possibly have a learning disability. In a case like this, you could use graphic organizers like story maps for fiction books and KWL charts for nonfiction books. I have included many of these at the back of this book. I will also discuss them in more detail in upcoming chapters, specifically Chapter Nine—Retell Chart (Form D).

Section Six: Interventions Used

Figure 3.6

Interventions Used:

This section (figure 3.6) is a listing of all the interventions that are being used for that particular student. Other interventions could include decodable readers, sight word flashcards, repeated reading, etc. This makes it easy to keep track of what you are using. This way the parents know exactly what is being used. Other teachers who work with the student will also know what is being used.

Using the Student Progress Monitoring Report (Form A) to Help Plan Future Interventions

I like to think of the Student Progress Monitoring Report (Form A) as a composite of many different sources of data. All of this important information is included on one page. This allows for easy analysis of your data. Use this data to answer questions such as:

Is there a notable improvement from the previous weeks?

If there is a notable improvement, this would suggest that the interventions being used are working. If there isn't, perhaps other interventions should be tried. Or maybe the interventions you have been using could be modified in some way. For example, maybe words per minute increased a lot at first but then slowed down. The student has improved. However, they are still below benchmark. Reflect on what is being done. You have been doing repeated reading twice a week at 15 minutes each time. A suggestion would be to keep doing it because it was working, but add another day or session.

What areas are improving?

This will give us an overall idea if the interventions are working. If not, we have a better idea of what to work on.

What interventions seem to be working?

Use your judgement to decide on what you think is working.

Can we add more of this intervention?

Ask yourself how to incorporate more of the successful interventions.

Are any areas not improving?

If there are areas that are not improving, take a good look at what you are doing. Is there a reason it may not be working?

What interventions could you add or change?

Is there something different you can try?

Does the student appear to be on pace to reach year-end goals?

If so, continue what you are doing. If not, consider adding additional interventions per week.

Do I need to make different goals for the student? Do we need to increase or decrease the student's goals?

It may be possible that the goals you have set for the students are too high. If you feel that they are not improving at an adequate rate, you may need to lower the goals so that the student can feel the success of reaching goals.

Chapter Four

Progress Monitoring Student Report (Form A) - Example

(Or "Let's take a look at how this student is doing.")

Let's start by looking at the Progress Monitoring Student Form (A) for this student after the fall DIBELS is administered.

Example
Progress Monitoring Student Form (A)

DIBELS Results-September: *(underlined if benchmark was met)*

LNF (letter naming fluency)	PSF (phoneme segmentation fluency)	NWF (nonsense word fluency)	Composite
No benchmark	40-benchmark	27/1-benchmark	113
18	47	15/0	80

STAR and SEL: *(Key: urg.=needs extra intervention , int.=needs intervention, OW=on watch (may need intervention), at=at or above benchmark)*

	STAR(SS, GE & IRL)	SEL	Baseline (total and alt. baseline)
#1	68 (int.), 1.0, PP	602-int.	67%/0 words

Progress Monitoring: *(underlined means first benchmark met, * Means 2nd met, ^ means 3rd met, numbers in () indicate difference from last DIB)*

	LNF	PSF (40)	NWF (27/1)	ORF	Retell #/qual	Accuracy
#1	-	-	20/5	3 WPM	0/0	5 errors
#2	-	-	20/2	1 WPM	0/0	7 errors

AR: *(as of 9/23/17)*

Total Points	%	Level
0 points	-	-

Interventions Used: *Phonics Dance (for decoding words with digraphs)/37 most common chunks (for help with decoding and word recognition)/iPad apps that focus on decoding such as Starfall and Reading Magic/ Snap Words (for rapid recognition of sight words)/Various decodable readers (for decoding practice and fluency)*

Key: *NWF-reading made-up words ORF-oral reading fluency (how many words read in a minute) Composite-a combination score of all the areas. Retell # and quality-How many words and how many details—4 is best for quality. STAR and SEL-these are exams that test comprehension and other skills GE-grade equivalent—what level they tested IRL-instructional reading level, the level that they should read at to improve (not too easy and not too hard).*

Let's Take a Look!

Let's start by taking a look at September DIBELS benchmark scores.

Figure 4.1

Dibels Results-September: *(underlined if benchmark was met)*

LNF (letter naming fluency)	PSF (phoneme segmentation fluency)	NWF (nonsense word fluency)	Composite
No benchmark	40-benchmark	27/1-benchmark	113
18	47	15/0	80

This is a Progress Monitoring Student Report (Form A) for a first grader we will call "Jane." By looking at the September DIBELS results, we hope to get an idea of what the ability level of this student is. This assessment was given at the beginning of the school year. If the student is new to us, this will provide valuable information. Even if we are aware of a student's skills from the previous year, inactivity during the summer may have hurt them.

For the **letter naming fluency (LNF)**, Jane scored an 18. This means 18 letters were recognized in one minute. While there is no benchmark for LNF, this number is low considering that the time allowed for this assessment was 60 seconds. With this in mind, we need to note that Jane needs extra help in the area of letter recognition. Hopefully, her letter recognition is something that will increase fairly quickly. The low number may be due to inactivity during the summer.

Next we will look at the **phoneme segmentation fluency (PSF)**. This assessment is given to check the student's ability to take a word and separate it into the smallest phonemic segments possible. The words given are actual one syllable words. The benchmark for the first administration is 40 correct sounds. Jane's score was 47 correct sounds. This would suggest to us that she has fair ability in this area.

Nonsense word fluency (NWF) is next. The first number is the number of correct sounds decoded. The student scored a 15 and the benchmark is 27. The student's score is significantly lower than the benchmark. Therefore the student could benefit from extra intervention. We will take note of this. Possible intervention will be discussed more in Chapter 6. The second number is the amount of whole words read. Jane scored a 0 and the benchmark is 1. Again, this is definitely an area that needs to be addressed and monitored.

The final score is the composite score. This is a combination of all the assessments. Jane scored an 80 and the benchmark is a 113.

Summary of the Fall Assessment:

Overall, the results suggest Jane is a good fit for extra reading intervention. Further analysis suggests that intervention should be focused on decoding. Also, we need to keep an eye on her letter recognition skills. This knowledge gives us a good starting point when planning our interventions.

Let's look at the Progress Monitoring Student Form (A) for Jane after the winter administration of DIBELS. *[That this is what the Progress Monitoring Student Form (A) will look like when the winter DIBELS is administered.]*

Example
Progress Monitoring Student Form (A)

DIBELS Results-January *(* means winter benchmark met)*

NWF (nonsense word fluency) 43/8-benchmark	ORF 23-benchmark	Retell n/a	Accuracy 78%	Composite 130- benchmark
54*/15*	14 WPM	4	78%	139*

DIBELS Results-September *(underlined if benchmark was met)*

LNF (letter naming fluency) No benchmark	PSF (phoneme segmentation fluency) 40-benchmark	NWF (nonsense word fluency) 27/1-benchmark	Composite 113
18	47	15/0	80

STAR and SEL *(Key: urg.=needs extra intervention, int.=needs intervention, OW=on watch (may need intervention), at=at or above benchmark)*

	STAR(SS, GE & IRL)	SEL	Baseline (total and alt. baseline)
#1	68 (int.), 1.0, PP	602-int.	67%/0 words
#2	72 (int.), 1.1, PP	692-at	-

Progress Monitoring: *(underlined means first benchmark met, * Means 2nd met, ^ means 3rd met, numbers in () indicate difference from last DIB)*

	LNF	PSF (40)	NWF (58/13)	ORF (47)	Retell #/ qual (15)	Accuracy
#1	-	-	20/5	3 WPM	0/0	5 errors
#2	-	-	20/2	1 WPM	0/0	7 errors
#3	-	-	24/3	4 WPM	1/1	6 errors
#4	-	-	23/5	0 WPM	1/1	8 errors
#5	-	-	29/7	1 WPM	1/1	6 errors
#6	-	-	26/5	1 WPM	1/1	6 errors
#7	-	-	27/6	6 WPM	2/1	5 errors
#8	-	-	36/8*	11 WPM	3/1	5 errors
#9	-	-	31/8*	11 WPM	5/1	5 errors
#10	-	-	41/12*	10 WPM	1/1	4 errors

AR: *(as of 1/11/17)*

Total Points	%	Level
7.8 points	63.7%	1.6

Interventions Used: *Phonics Dance (for decoding words with digraphs)/37 most common chunks (for help with decoding and word recognition)/iPad apps that focus on decoding such as Starfall and Reading Magic/ Snap Words (for rapid recognition of sight words)/Various decodable readers (for decoding practice and fluency)*

Key: *NWF-reading made-up words ORF-oral reading fluency (how many words read in a minute) **Composite**-a combination score of all the areas. **Retell # and quality**-how many words and how many details—4 is best for quality. **STAR and SEL**-these are exams that test comprehension and other skills **GE**-grade equivalent, what level they tested **IRL**-instructional reading level, the level that they should read at to improve (not too easy and not too hard).*

Let's first focus on the winter administration of the DIBELS.

Figure 4.2

DIBELS Results-January *(* means winter benchmark met)*

NWF (nonsense word fluency)	ORF	Retell	Accuracy	Composite
43/8-benchmark	23-benchmark	n/a	78%	130- benchmark
54*/15*	14 WPM	4/1	78%	139*

Notice that LNF and PSF are not given during this administration. Let's focus on the NWF. You will notice that the benchmark rose from 27/1 to 43/15. Our student, Jane, scored a 54/15. The * signifies that she reached benchmark. This was up from the 15/0 score of last time. That fact that she reached benchmark and improved greatly suggests that instruction is going very well for this student. The high second number tells me that she is recognizing and saying the whole word. Let's look at the weekly progress monitoring scores up to this point.

Figure 4.3

NWF (43/8)
20/5
20/2
24/3
23/5
29/7
26/5
27/6
36/8*
31/8*
41/12*

If the weekly progress monitoring scores are consistently high, I would feel comfortable stopping the weekly progress monitoring score for NWF. Next we will look at the ORF. This was not given during the fall. She scored 14 WPM. The benchmark is 23 words per minute. She did not reach benchmark. This needs our attention. Possible intervention will be discussed more in Chapter 8. However, this is still fairly new to first grade so we will carefully keep watch on how she improves. I would like to note that even though ORF was not given in September, I started progress monitoring right away. The purpose of this is to give me an idea of what her decoding abilities are while reading a passage at this point in the year.

Next is the retell. The retell score involves 2 numbers separated by a slash. The first number is the total number of words that the student retold. The words counted had to have something to do with the story that they read. The next number is the quality of the retell. Quality is rated on a scale of 1 to 4. A 1 means they didn't remember very much, and a 4 means they remembered at least three good things in a logical order while giving the main idea. There's not a benchmark for the winter administration. We saw that our student's score is 4/1. This means that she said 4 things about the story and the quality was very low. This is something they need to work on despite there being no benchmark. The reason that there is no benchmark is because the focus this early on is on correctly reading the words. As we just saw, her ORF is lower than benchmark, so the retell will not improve until that does. To give an idea of what expected improvement should be, the next benchmark is 15 words retold. Possible interventions for comprehension will be discussed more in Chapter 10.

Our next area of assessment is accuracy. This is the total percentage of words correct. The benchmark is 78%. This is a fairly low percentage, but reading a whole passage is still a new experience for many first graders. Our student scored an accuracy rate of 78%. This would suggest she is on the right track as far as accuracy goes. The next benchmark in spring jumps up to 90%.

Finally we have our composite score. This score is a combination of all the scores to give an overall view of ability. The student scored a 139 and the benchmark is a 130. This is above benchmark. However, I view this score with caution. The reason behind this is because a really high score in one area can inflate the score and may suggest the student is at a higher ability than they actually are.

Summary of the winter assessment:

Overall, Jane is showing improvement. The NWF score suggests her basic decoding skills are coming along at a good rate. I can back this up with everyday observation of her participation in class. Her ORF is low and needs proper intervention. However, I am encouraged by her accuracy rate. We will focus on improving her fluency. There are a number of activities I will discuss later that can help to improve fluency. Her retell, which is a reflection of her comprehension, needs work. The priority should be improving her fluency. The stronger the fluency, the stronger the comprehension. However, there are still comprehension activities that can be done. I will describe these later.

On the next page is the Progress Monitoring Student Report (Form A) shown after the spring administration of DIBELS. Let's look at the Progress Monitoring Student Form (A) for the same student after the spring administration of DIBELS.

Example
Progress Monitoring Student Form (A)

DIBELS Results-April *(^ means spring benchmark met)*

NWF (nonsense word fluency) 58/13-benchmark	ORF 47-benchmark	Retell (# and quality) 15-benchmark	Accuracy 90%	Composite 155-benchmark
56/15^	37 WPM	12/1	93%^	154

DIBELS Results-January *(* means winter benchmark met)*

NWF (nonsense word fluency) 43/8-benchmark	ORF 23-benchmark	Retell n/a	Accuracy 78%	Composite 130-benchmark
54*/15*	14 WPM	4	78%	139*

DIBELS Results-September *(underlined if benchmark was met)*

LNF (letter naming fluency) No benchmark	PSF (phoneme segmentation fluency) 40-benchmark	NWF (nonsense word fluency) 27/1-benchmark	Composite 113
18	47	15/0	80

STAR and SEL: *(Key: urg.=needs extra intervention , int.=needs intervention, OW=on watch (may need intervention), at=at or above benchmark)*

	STAR (SS, GE & IRL)	SEL	Baseline (total and alt. baseline)
#1	68 (int.), 1.0, PP	602-int.	67%/0 words
#2	72 (int.), 1.1, PP	692-at	-
#3	63 (urg.), 1.0, PP	782-at	-
#4	80 (int.), 1.2, PP	?	-

Progress Monitoring: *(underlined means first benchmark met, * Means 2nd met, ^ means 3rd met, numbers in () indicate difference from last DIB)*

	LNF	PSF (40)	NWF (58/13)	ORF (47)	Retell #/qual (15)	Accuracy
#1	-	-	20/5	3 WPM	0/0	5 errors
#2	-	-	20/2	1 WPM	0/0	7 errors
#3	-	-	24/3	4 WPM	1/1	6 errors
#4	-	-	23/5	0 WPM	1/1	8 errors
#5	-	-	29/7	1 WPM	1/1	6 errors
#6	-	-	26/5	1 WPM	1/1	6 errors
#7	-	-	27/6	6 WPM	2/1	5 errors
#8	-	-	36/8*	11 WPM	3/1	5 errors
#9	-	-	31/8*	11 WPM	5/1	5 errors
#10	-	-	41/12*	10 WPM	1/1	4 errors
#11	-	-	-	20 WPM	8/1	5 errors
#12	-	-	-	21 WPM	5/1	4 errors
#13	-	-	-	37 WPM	8/1	4 errors
#14	-	-	-	21 WPM	7/1	5 errors
#15	-	-	-	35 WPM	10/1	3 errors
#16	-	-	-	40 WPM	13/1	1 error

AR: *(as of 4/11/17)*

Total Points	%	Level
28.8 points	63.7%	1.6

Interventions Used: *Phonics Dance (for decoding words with digraphs)/37 most common chunks (for help with decoding and word recognition)/iPad apps that focus on decoding such as Starfall and Reading Magic/ Snap Words (for rapid recognition of sight words)/Various decodable readers (for decoding practice and fluency)*

Let's look at the spring DIBELS results for the same student:

Figure 4.4
DIBELS Results-April *(^ means spring benchmark met)*

NWF (nonsense word fluency) 58/13-benchmark	ORF 47-benchmark	Retell (# and quality) 15-benchmark	Accuracy 90%	Composite 155-benchmark
56/15^	37 WPM	12/1	93%^	154

Let's first look at the NWF. The benchmark has risen to 58/13. The first number is the total correct letter sounds. Jane's score is a 56, so it is a little less than benchmark. Last time, she scored above benchmark. Even though she is below benchmark, it doesn't concern me too much. This feeling is also due to the fact that she scored above benchmark in the whole words read. The benchmark was a 13 and she scored a 15.

Next is the ORF. She scored a 37 WPM with the benchmark being 47 WPM. Just like last time, she was below benchmark and we need to be aware of this. I don't see this as a major red flag because she did improve a lot from the winter administration. However, we need to increase her fluency intervention to make up ground.

Retell is our next focus. This time the benchmark for total words retold is 15. She received a 12. Therefore, she did not reach benchmark. For the last administration, there was no benchmark because of the idea we need to improve fluency. We need to add more and more comprehension strategies. Her score for quality was a 1. Benchmark is a 2. This means she retold less than three relevant details.

Accuracy is our next area to look at. The benchmark is now 90%. Our student scored a 93%. This is a good sign. Even though her ORF was below the benchmark, the high accuracy rate suggests she might be scoring lower as a result of taking her time decoding. This is a good sign that she will respond well to fluency intervention. Increased intervention will likely be needed to improve comprehension.

Finally, we have our composite or overall score. Her composite was just one point under benchmark. As stated earlier, I am cautious when dealing with the composite score because it can be skewed by a really high score or a really low score in one area. It still is good to take note of the composite score to see if it is really high or really low.

Summary of the spring assessment:
Overall our student is showing improvement, but is still below benchmark. The positive finding to take from this DIBELS is that her NWF and accuracy scores indicate good decoding skills. The negative findings are that her fluency and comprehension need work. However, both areas are much higher than before. Her progress monitoring scores taken around this time support these findings.

Chapter Five

Nonsense Word Table (Form B)

(Or "How do we know what sounds are being missed?")

In this chapter, we will discuss the Nonsense Word Table (Form B).

Figure 5.1

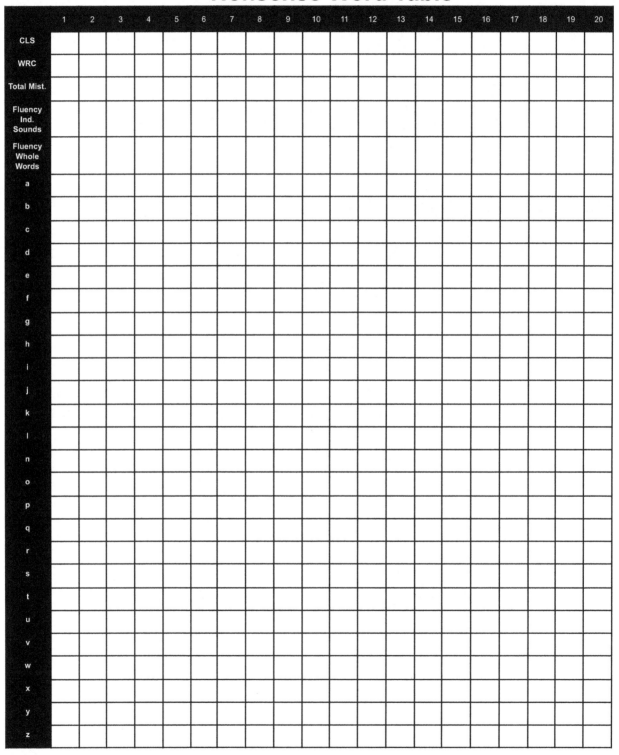

Nonsense Word Table

	1	2	3	4	5	6	7	8	9	10	11	12	13	14	15	16	17	18	19	20
CLS																				
WRC																				
Total Mist.																				
Fluency Ind. Sounds																				
Fluency Whole Words																				
a																				
b																				
c																				
d																				
e																				
f																				
g																				
h																				
i																				
j																				
k																				
l																				
n																				
o																				
p																				
q																				
r																				
s																				
t																				
u																				
v																				
w																				
x																				
y																				
z																				

Name:

This table (fig 5.1) is to help us track a student's basic decoding by analyzing their nonsense word fluency (NWF). As stated previously, NWF tracks the student's ability to decode simple, made-up words. If the student scores below benchmark on DIBELS, we will progress monitor this on a weekly basis. You should also use this if you notice a student struggling while reading basic decodable words. This table takes a closer look at what types and patterns of mistakes are made. This helps pinpoint areas of weakness so that interventions can be properly selected. The chart was specifically made for the progress monitoring booklets that come with the DIBELS assessment. However, you could just as easily use the chart with any assessment that follows these guidelines:

1. *List of several made-up words that can be separated into three phonemes. (for example, hec, nof, etc.) The words can sound like real words as long as they are not spelled correctly.*

2. *The words must contain a wide variety of consonant sounds and vowel sounds. Ideally all the letters should be represented.*

3. *The time given for the student to read is one minute.*

4. *Different words are used with each administration.*

The main reason for this chart is to look for patterns. We need to know what kind of errors the student is making, not just that they are making errors. Common patterns you might notice are saying "B" instead of "D," "P" instead of "Q," "M" instead of "W," "Z" instead of "S." You might also notice a type of recurring error that is unique to the individual. Another common type of error has to do with vowels. If we track which vowels the reader is having trouble with, we will be able to more effectively plan interventions. Using this chart will make you more efficient and productive during your time spent working on sounds.

Parts of the Nonsense Word Table (Form B)

CLS (Correct Letter Sounds): The CLS is the total number of sounds pronounced correctly. If the word was "nok," the student could say each sound with a pause and it would be correct. This is to measure the ability to recognize letters and their sounds. However, it is not indicative of whether or not they can put the sounds together to make a whole word. So while it can give an indication if they know their sounds, it does not tell whether or not they can decode more than one sound together. The next row will.

WRC (Words Read Correctly): The WRC is the amount of words that are read completely blended together. This number is an indicator of how good the student is with decoding complete words smoothly. They must read the word with no hesitation to count as a whole word read.

Total Mistakes: The total number of mistakes. This is an often overlooked part of the nonsense word fluency assessment. Often, the CLS and WRC are looked at as the best indicators. However, in my experiences I have seen many students have CLS scores and high WRC scores but several errors. A quick glance would make it seem that the reader might be satisfactory in this area, but it could also hide the fact that they may be making error patterns that need to be addressed.

Fluency Individual Sounds/Fluency Whole Words: The evaluator will check the "Fluency Individual Sounds" box if the student reads the word by sounding out each individual sound with a pause. They will check the "Fluency Whole Words" if they are able to read the whole blended word smoothly.

Letters: After the student is done reading, I put down a number representing how many of each letter was missed. If there were no mistakes, it is left blank.

Benefits of Using this Table

The biggest benefit is being able to pinpoint what kind of errors are being made during their decoding process. The fact that nonsense words are used instead of real words helps eliminate memorization. I have found that the following questions can be answered to some degree by using this chart:

What letters are the student most commonly missing?

Do they mix up short and long vowel sounds?

Do they often miss the last sound?

Is decoding automatic or do they have to sound it out? (This could either be sounding out each sound out loud or pausing and doing it in their head.)

Chapter Six

Nonsense Word Table (Form B) - Example

(Or "Is this student having trouble with particular letters?")

Let's take a look!

Here we have a NWF table of a first-grade student (fig. 6.1). We will call this student "Kevin." These are the letters that they missed while reading nonsense words. This is to give an idea of what letters need extra practice.

Figure 6.1

Nonsense Word Table

	1	2	3	4	5	6	7	8	9	10	11	12	13	14	15	16	17	18	19	20
CLS	23	31	31	33	64	61	52	33	39	30	50	42	57	58	46	48	70			
WRC	0	0	0	0	0	5	5	11	9	6	14	12	18	20	14	15	23			
Total Mist.	2	0	1	0	2	2	1	2	4	4	3	2	4	0	3	3	2			
Fluency Ind. Sounds	x	x	x	x	x	x	x													
Fluency Whole Words						x	x	x	x	x	x	x	x	x	x	x	x			
a											1									
b																				
c																				
d																				
e			1									2			2	1	2			
f																				
g																				
h																				
i													3			1				
j																				
k																				
l																				
m	1																			
n							1		2											
o						1		1	1	2	2		1							
p									1											
q																				
r																				
s						1														
t																				
u	1				1					1					1					
v																				
w																				
x																				
y																1				
z								1												

Name: Kevin

Correct Letter Sounds (CLS)

What we need to look at first is the CLS. We want to see how many correct sounds Kevin is saying. His weekly CLS scores are below.

Figure 6.2

	CLS
#1	23
#2	31
#3	31
#4	33
#5	64
#6	61
#7	52
#8	33
#9	39
#10	30
#11	50
#12	42
#13	57
#14	58
#15	46
#16	48
#17	70

Just a reminder that CLS stands for correct letter sounds. CLS does not take into account whether the words are read as a whole or not. I do not have the DIBELS benchmarks mentioned on these tables for a couple of reasons. One reason is because I use the chart throughout the year and it is hard to find a pertinent spot to put the benchmarks. However, one of the most important reasons I use this chart is to look for improvement. Therefore, the key is to look and see if the number is going up. For our student, Kevin, we see he has improved quite a bit from the first administration to the last. The interventions provided for Kevin are working, but there is still room for improvement.

One thing that catches my eye while looking at the CLS is that his scores, while improving, are also very inconsistent. He reaches the 60s and then goes down to the 30s. It is important to hypothesize why this is happening. One reason might be that he just had an off day. Maybe there was something else taking part in the room that distracted him. However, if his Words Read Correctly (WRC) are going up (see next section), it might not be a concern. Often times, a student's CLS will go down as they focus on saying the whole word. Sometimes going from sounding out every letter to reading the whole road can be a hard habit to break. The teacher may need to be patient and focus on the fact that the child is trying to take the next step and praise the small improvement.

Words Read Correctly (WRC)

Now we need to look at the words read correctly (fig. 6.3).

Figure 6.3

	WRC
#1	0
#2	0
#3	0
#4	0
#5	0
#6	5
#7	5
#8	11
#9	9
#10	6
#11	14
#12	12
#13	18
#14	20
#15	14
#16	15
#17	23

Let's take a look at how well Kevin is reading the word as a whole without orally sounding the individual sounds (fig. 6.3). At the beginning of the year, it took him awhile to get out of the habit of reading the sounds individually. He has increased on a fairly regular basis. He is doing well in this area.

Total Mistakes

Let's take a look at how many mistakes Kevin is making (fig 6.4).

Figure 6.4

	Total mis.
#1	2
#2	0
#3	1
#4	0
#5	2
#6	2
#7	1
#8	2

#9	4
#10	4
#11	3
#12	2
#13	4
#14	0
#15	3
#16	3
#17	2

Looking at Kevin's score, we see that he is somewhat inconsistent with errors. Sometimes he made no errors. There was one point where he made four errors twice in a row. The next section will give us a better idea of what types of errors Kevin is making and possibly give us an idea why he is making them. One of the first things I noticed was that the errors picked up after he started reading the words more as a whole. This could suggest that vowel sounds might be an issue because learning readers sometimes will say the long sound automatically and not the short vowel sound.

Fluency Individual Sounds and Fluency Whole Words

Let's take a look at whether Kevin is sounding out the words with individual sounds or as a whole word. (fig. 6.5)

Figure 6.5

Fluency Ind. Sounds	Fluency Whole Words
X	
X	
X	
X	
X	
X	X
X	X
	X
	X
	X
	X
	X
	X
	X
	X
	X
	X
	X

These two columns are "Fluency-Individual Sounds" and "Fluency Whole Words." If the student is reading individual sounds, the first column is marked. If the student reads the whole words without sounding it out, the second column is marked. Of course, we want the student to read the whole word. Kevin has been reading the whole words rather consistently. He started out the first grade year by reading each sound (or sounding out the made-up word). Kevin read each sound for 5 weeks. By the 6th week, with encouragement from myself, he started to read some of the words whole. Both columns are marked because he did a combination of reading the whole word and sounding it out.

The transitioning from sounding out every letter to sounding out the whole word can be a challenge. That is because it can be a hard habit to break. My belief is that often the student may feel that getting all the letters is good enough. I often will remind them to sound out the whole word in their head. Then I use this chart to put an emphasis on how many whole words they are able to read. This chart will give them proof in their minds that they are getting better. They will start to realize that they can get farther if they read the whole word.

Letters Missed

Now let's take a look at the specific letters the student missed (fig. 6.6).

Figure 6.6

a	b	c	d	e	f	g	h	i	j	k	l	m	n	o	p	q	r	s	t	u	v	w	x	y	z
											1								1						
				1																					
																			1						
														1			1								
								1																	
														1											1
													2	1	1										
														2				1							
1														2											
				2																					
							3							1											
				2														1							
				1				1															1		
				2																					

All the letters are included. I mark which letters are missed on my copy as the student reads the nonsense words to me. After the reading is complete, I mark how many of each letter was missed. This makes it easy to look for patterns and focus on more direct instruction. As we can see, Kevin is having problems with vowels. This is common at his age. A good intervention for Kevin could be using decodable readers that focus on the vowel sounds. Most reading series have decodable readers included in their program. The website Readinga-z.com also has an excellent supply of printable decodable readers.

Let's take a look at some other easy-to-use interventions for assisting with decoding.

Flash Cards: Make flash cards of nonsense words containing letters missed. Practice daily. As accuracy improves, encourage the student to read the whole word. This may take time. It is okay to have them pause and sound out the word in their heads as long as their lips don't move. As this improves, make flashcards with nonsense words. Encourage the student not to sound out the word orally. Give praise when they do it correctly. Make it clear to them that the goal is to read the whole word. You could then add real decodable words on flashcards with the task of having the student determine if it is a real word or not. Progress could be tracked by using a set number of cards (20, for example) and log the time it takes the student to read these.

Chunking: Another thing I have found that often works effectively is taking a chunk. This is simply a vowel and a consonant or consonants. Change the first letter quickly and have the student rhyme while looking at it. Doing this on a small white board works well. Using the most common chunks also works well (Wylie & Durrell, 1970). The common chunks are listed here in a table. I also have included a chart that I use to encourage "chunking" in Appendix 2.

Figure 6.7

ack	ap	ell	in	old	unk
ain	ash	est	ing	op	
ake	at	ice	ink	ore	
ale	ate	ick	ip	ot	
ame	aw	ide	it	uck	
an	ay	ight	ock	ug	
ank	eat	ill	oke	ump	

Chunk Card Activities

Onset and rime pieces to use with these activities are included at the end of this chapter.

Chunk Match: For this activity, you have a set of onsets (beginnings) and rimes (chunks). The student pulls an onset out of the onset envelope and then pulls a chunk out of the chunk envelope. The two parts are put together and the student decodes the whole word and signifies whether it is a real word or not. Onset and rime pieces are included at the end of this chapter.

Simply cut them out and keep the onset and rime pieces separated by storing them in different envelopes.

Flashcards: Lay all the chunk pieces face up in one pile and all the beginning ones face up in another pile. They should be spread out a little. You can then point to each piece and have your student name them as quickly as they can. You could set the missed one aside and work on those some more.

Make a word: Put the beginning pieces face down in one pile and put the chunk pieces face down in another pile. Your child will grab a beginning piece and then a chunk piece and put them together. They will then say the word. If they read the new word correctly, they get a point. If they make a real word, they get another point. Continue until all the pieces are used. They can try for a high score each time.

Word substitution: Put all the beginning pieces and chunk pieces face up in different piles. Have the student make a real word. For example, they could make the word "crack." Challenge the student to make a new real word by changing the chunk. For example, you could change the "ack" to "ank" to make "crank." Then change the beginning piece to make another word. For example, "cr" to "bl" to make "blank." Continue alternating between the chunks and beginnings until you can't make any more words. You can also practice using each word in a sentence to practice vocabulary.

Word Flower

A good way to practice decoding and manipulating the middle sounds of words is to write a one syllable word inside a circle on an erasable board. Leave the vowel blank. Draw five lines coming out from the circle with a circle at the end of each line. Write a vowel in each circle. Write "a" in the blank space of the word. Have the student read the word and determine if it is a real word or not. Continue this with the remaining four vowels.

Figure 6.8

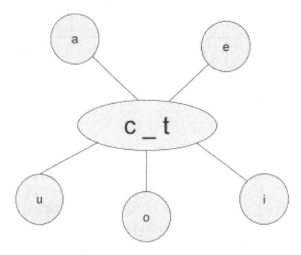

Onsets for game

ch	st	cl	b	k
sh	sm	dr	c	l
ph	sp	gl	d	m
kn	fl	gr	f	n
th	bl	pr	g	p
wh	br	pl	h	qu
sl	cr	tr	j	r
s	t	v	w	z

Rimes (chunks) for game

ack	ap	ell	in
ain	ash	est	ing
ake	at	ice	ink
ale	ate	ick	ip
ame	aw	ide	it
an	ay	ight	ock
ank	eat	ill	oke
old	op	ore	ot
uck	ug	unk	

Chapter Seven

Fluency Chart (Form C)

(Or "Does this student read smoothly or choppily?")

In this chapter, we will discuss the Fluency Chart (Form C).

This graph contains the weekly progress monitoring scores.

	1	2	3	4	5	6	7	8	9	10	11	12	13	14	15	16	17	18	19
70 and over																			
68																			
66																			
64																			
62																			
60																			
58																			
56																			
54																			
52																			
50																			
48																			
Spring																			
46																			
44																			
42																			
40																			
38																			
36																			
34																			
32																			
30																			
28																			
26																			
24																			
Win bench																			
22																			
20																			
18																			
16																			
14																			
12																			
10																			
8																			
6																			
4																			
WPM																			

*means they had an odd number of words per minute, so add one word to the total. Example, if the bar goes up to 20 and there is a *, the total is 21. The first bold line is the winter benchmark and the second one is the spring benchmark

Name_____

Fluency Chart (Form C)

The Fluency Chart (Form C) is one of my favorites. I know there are many tables out there, but I initially had trouble finding one to fit my needs. With this in mind, I developed some and adjusted them over the years. Most importantly, I wanted something appealing to the student and the parent also. It needed to be something easy to use and understand. The table shown on the previous page is one of many charts that I use. I want to make it clear that this is one I use for first graders, but I have included charts for other grades at the end of this book. These charts can also be found at www.foustreading.simplesite.com. Remember that the charts can be adjusted.

This bar graph has several uses. Of course, one use is to display our data. However, a big difference between this and other ways of displaying data is the motivation it provides. Motivation of the student is a driving force behind this graph. It allows the student to see improvement as it is happening. I have found that students really enjoy looking at this graph around once a week. If time allows, I will have the students add to the graph as soon as the one-minute reading is administered. While there are templates at www.foustreading.simplesite.com, I have also included blank graphs you can fill out by hand. These forms are located at the back of this book. These charts do not take much time and give the students something to strive for. These allow the students to see their progress towards a goal. This table especially appeals to competitive kids.

Another good use of this chart is to show progress (or lack of progress) to the parents. Just displaying numbers and data might not be enough for parents or others to visualize improvement. This graph goes a long way in helping parents see how their child is progressing. This table also includes the DIBELS benchmarks. My students' parents really like having a visual way to see how their children are progressing toward their goals. The benchmark lines could easily be changed to specific word per minute goals. Or you could simply remove them.

Teacher use, of course, is another use of the chart. This is true especially in the area of fluency. The chart is an easy way to track rate and speed. I can take a quick glance and know if my fluency interventions are working.

Features of the Chart

Words Per Minute (WPM)- On this chart, the WPM are on the left side. These run up the left side of the chart.

Student scores- A place for the student WPM scores is at the bottom of the chart. This includes their weekly progress monitoring scores and can include the official DIBELS scores. Often, I will make the bars of the DIBELS scores in black to stand out. I use different colors for the weekly progress monitoring scores. As stated previously, I try to progress monitor once a week to obtain these scores. Typically this is on a Friday. These are one-minute timings.

Benchmark lines- These are bold, thick lines on the chart to show fall, winter, and spring benchmarks. I feel this is a good visual for the students to see the score that they need to aim for. You can also use a different number if the DIBELS benchmark score is too easy or too hard for that particular student.

Fluency Scale

Below is my fluency scale. I don't have a place for it on this particular chart. However, it is important to have some sort of way to rate fluency. It will also be used on another chart that we will look at soon.

1. Slow, like a robot. Sounds out words.
2. OK, but still a little slow. May sound out a word or two.
3. Pretty good.
4. Perfect! Sounds like the student is talking. Not too fast and not too slow. Reads with expression.

One thing I like about using this scale is that it gives the student a goal. This goal can be used at different times when the students are orally reading. If the difficulty of the passage is high, do not give a number directly to the student. I typically only give the students their number if they have practiced the passage or it is somewhat easy for them. You do not want them to get discouraged. However, I will often record their fluency of a first-time read without telling them the score. In my opinion, it is a very good way to compare fluency improvement over time.

Chapter Eight

Fluency Chart (Form C) - Example

(or "Is this student a 'smooth reader'?")

Let's take a look!

Here we have a fluency chart of a first-grade student. We will call this student "Quinn."

WPM	3	1	4	0	1	1	6	11	11	10	14	20	21	37	21	37	40	37
#	1	2	3	4	5	6	7	8	9	10	DIB	11	12	13	14	15	16	DIB

*means they had an odd number of words per minute, so add one word to the total. Example, if the bar goes up to 20 and there is a *, the total is 21. The first bold line is the winter benchmark and the second one is the spring benchmark.*

Name: Quinn

Let's Take a Look!

This is the bar graph of all the ORF progress monitoring scores for Quinn. This Fluency Chart (Form C) is from the end of the year. The black ones are the official DIBELS scores. The DIBELS scores are included so you can easily compare the weekly progress monitoring scores to them. Notice that there is not a DIBELS score at the beginning. The reason for this is because this example was given to a first grader and DIBELS does not include an ORF assessment for the fall administration.

This student has shown much improvement. However, she is still below benchmark for the winter and spring. Even though she is below benchmark, the data does suggest that this student is making progress and on the right track.

What if the pattern is erratic?

At times there might be a pattern that doesn't seem like it makes sense. An example of this might be a bar graph with scores that are going up and then have an unusually steep decline. Then it might go right back up. One good thing about using a bar graph like this is that we have a large sample size. This helps us to not be too concerned if we see a big drop.

One reason for a low score might be that the student found the passage more difficult even though it is near the same reading level. They might have encountered a word or two that threw off their rhythm. I have noticed that some students have trouble bouncing back from mistakes. This might be a confidence issue. If you feel this might be the case, reading some easier passages may boost their confidence.

Another possible cause might be that there was a distraction during testing. Is there something happening that they wanted to attend to? If you feel this might be the case, try testing them again by themselves. Or they might be tired, which will hurt their concentration. If you feel this might be the case, try testing them at a different point in the day.

Interest level could also have an effect on their score. Switching between fiction and non-fiction stories might be a reason for a lower score. I have often noticed that students score lower on non-fiction stories.

Possible interventions:

Looking at the data for this student would suggest she needs fluency practice. Let's look at an intervention that could work wonders to improve fluency. Normally, I would list several activities. However, you can do repeated reading on so many kinds of passages and in different ways. Repeated reading has been shown to improve fluency (Samuels, 2002). Repeated reading is simply taking a passage and reading it several times. The most important thing to keep in mind is that you carefully select and perform repeated reading in the following ways.

First of all, *find a good passage to use.* The passage should be at the student's independent reading level. This is the level that the student can read with very few mistakes. I personally find that poems work great for this. Poems that allow for different intonations are best. For example, poems with questions and exclamation sentences are a good choice as they allow for varied voice expression. The passage could also be a page from a storybook from the student's independent level. A passage of about 100 words will work well.

Have the student read the passage for you. Since it should be at the student's independent level, there should not be many mistakes. If there are mistakes, use the opportunity to practice the decoding skills described earlier.

Model the passage for the student. Use proper speed and expression. I often read it with them three times. Make sure that the student is following along. I have them point. Their eyes should be on it. This is important because if they aren't looking at the words, it won't have the desired effect. After the first time, have them read out loud with you.

Have them read the passage out loud. I find three or four repetitions are usually good. Again, make sure that they are actually looking at and reading the words.

Finally, have the student read it to you a final time. Give them a score from the fluency scale. If they do not get a 3 or 4, have them practice a little more. The scale is repeated below.

1. Slow, like a robot. Sounds out words.
2. OK, but still a little slow. May sound out a word or two.
3. Pretty good.
4. Perfect! Sounds like the student is talking. Not too fast and not too slow. Reads with expression.

Chapter Nine

Retell Chart (Form D)

(Or "Can a student remember and retell what they read?")

Let's Take a Look!

In this chapter, we will discuss the Retelling Chart (Form D).

Retelling

	Score	Very few details	3 or more details	3 or more details in order	3 or more details in order which also tell the main idea
DIBELS					
Progress Monitoring #1					
Progress Monitoring #2					
Progress Monitoring #3					
Progress Monitoring #4					
Progress Monitoring #5					
Progress Monitoring #6					
Progress Monitoring #7					
Progress Monitoring #8					
Progress Monitoring #9					

The Retell Chart (Form D) is something I started using recently. I was finding it difficult to convey the importance of a good retelling to some of my students. It was hard to get some students to focus on remembering what they read. Reading quickly was the most important task for them. As stated previously, I feel fluency is incredibly important. However, young readers need to learn that there is much more to being a good reader than just reading quickly.

Features of the Chart

This chart helped some of my students visualize many important facts or events from what they read. The scale that I use has been adapted from the comprehension scale used by DIBELS. Like fluency, I use a scale of 1 to 4. A 1 means that very few details were given (usually one or two). A 2 means three details or more were given, but not in sequential order and not too descriptive. A 3 means that three or more important details were given in sequential order. A 4 means that three or more details were given and the retelling really gives a good idea of what the main idea is.

Since I started using this chart, I have noticed a big improvement in many of my students. Many of these students were stuck in the idea that reading quickly is the only sign of a good reader. Of course, we want the good retelling to go beyond just the one-minute checks. Therefore, some kind of intervention has to be implemented that they can use in their normal everyday reading. In the next chapter, after we look at an example, I will share some graphic organizers that I utilize in my class.

Chapter Ten

Retell Chart (Form D) - Example

(Or "How well does this student retell what they read?")

Here we have a Retell Chart (Form D) of a second-grade student. We will call this student "James."

Figure 10.1

Retelling

	Score	Very few details	3 or more details	3 or more details in order	3 or more details in order which also tell the main idea
DIBELS	1 of 4				
Progress Monitoring #1	1 of 4				
Progress Monitoring #2	1 of 4				
Progress Monitoring #3	2 of 4				
Progress Monitoring #4	2 of 4				
Progress Monitoring #5	2 of 4				
Progress Monitoring #6	2 of 4				
Progress Monitoring #7	2 of 4				
Progress Monitoring #8	3 of 4				
Progress Monitoring #9	2 of 4				
Progress Monitoring #10	3 of 4				
Progress Monitoring #11	3 of 4				
Progress Monitoring #12	2 of 4				
Progress Monitoring #13	3 of 4				
Progress Monitoring #14	2 of 4				
Progress Monitoring #15	2 of 4				
Progress Monitoring #16	3 of 4				
Progress Monitoring #17	3 of 4				
Progress Monitoring #18	3 of 4				
Progress Monitoring #19	3 of 4				
Progress Monitoring #20	3 of 4				
Progress Monitoring #21					
Progress Monitoring #22					
Progress Monitoring #23					

Name: James

James was a student whom I was very concerned about at the beginning of the year. He improved his fluency from first grade to second grade. I just could not get through to him that he needed to remember what he had read. Eventually, his retell scores improved. James needed a visual aid. After a while, I added another visual effect for him. For this, I needed a bowl and some beads. When James (and my other students) gave me a retell, I would put a bead inside the bowl for each detail I was told (see figure 10.2). This activity wasn't limited to progress monitoring. I used it during regular reading instruction also.

Figure 10.2

James really took a liking to looking at the graph. As you can see, he went from very poor retellings at the beginning of the year to much better retelling at the end of the year. However, he has not reached 4 yet and there is more room for improvement. Let's take a look at a few interventions and tools that we can use to make James and our other students more aware of the details that are being read. Each graphic organizer mentioned here will also be in Appendix 2.

Possible Interventions

Story Map:

Figure 10.3

Story Map

Setting:

Characters: *(who)*
Who is the main character?

Problem:
Why did the problem happen?

Events: 1. 2. 3. 4. 5. 6. 7. 8. 9. 10.

Solution:

Ending:

Story maps are simply graphic organizers with sections for each major part of a story. These work best with fiction books. First, I introduce the story map to my class. I carefully go over it with them for the books we are reading in class. Slowly I start asking them to give me the parts without too much assistance. Even though I often give them copies they can write on, we do not spend a whole lot of time on that. Often I will have them tell me all the parts of a book before they are allowed to take an Accelerated Reader test. The idea is that we practice finding all the parts so many times that, as they are reading independently, the parts will be easy to recognize for them, almost like a light bulb coming on when they find one. These are also good for parents to have at home.

Summary Hand:

Figure 10.4

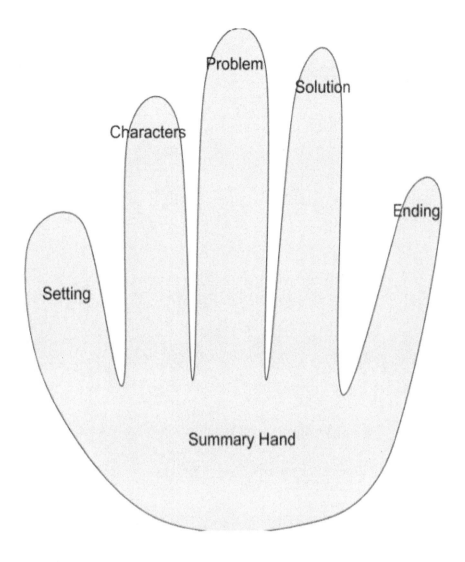

I use the summary hand in much the same way as the story map. We use it with fiction books. Often I will rotate using each one just to keep some variety. In my experience, some students react better to one or the other.

Chapter Eleven

One-Minute Reading Breakdown Chart (Form E)

(Or "How many things can we learn from a one-minute reading?")

In this chapter, we will discuss the One-Minute Reading Breakdown Chart (Form D).

One Minute Reading Breakdown

	A	B	C	D	E	F	G	H	I	J	K	L	M	N	O
	total words	total errors	sight words errors (words that don't sound out)	fluency (1-4)	problems chunking (clarifying)- these are words that sound out	mispronounced (first sound right, but ending wrong)	substitutions (completely different word, guessed based on words around it)	pronounced to students (did not attempt orally)	Do mistakes change meaning? (Is it the same part of speech or does it make sense?)	retelling (1-4), How many important details were retold? 4 is the best	hesitations, but correct decoding skills? 4 is the best	decoding skills (1-4) How well did they decode/chunk/sound out? How good were their decoding skills? 4 is the best	multi-syllable with incorrect vowel (How many words with incorrect vowel sounds)	trouble with short vowel sounds (How many short vowel sounds did they miss?)	Trouble with long vowel sounds (How many long vowel words did they miss?)
#1				out of 4											
#2															
#3															
#4															
#5															
#6															
#7										out of 4					
#8												out of 4			
#9															
#10															
#11															
	fluency	accuracy	word recognition and fluency	fluency	decoding	decoding	decoding	comprehension/context clues	comprehension	decoding and fluency	decoding and fluency	decoding and fluency	decoding	decoding	decoding

What do the different columns mean?

A-This is words per minute. We want to see this number go up. The goal for first grade at the end of the year is 47. B-Errors-This is total mistakes. We want to see this go down. Even just one or two is an improvement. This is also called accuracy. C-Sight words-These are words that don't sound out. D-This is fluency (accuracy, speed, and tone of voice). A 1 is like a robot and a 4 is just like you are talking. E-Chunking-These are words that the student should know how to clarify if given time. F-Mispronounced. These mistakes usually involve the student looking at the first letter and guessing. G-Substitutions-These mistakes usually mean that the student guessed what would be next without really looking. H- With these errors, the students were given about three seconds and couldn't make a guess, so they were told the word. I- A mistake that "changes meaning" is a mistake that doesn't make sense, but the student continues on. J-This is what they remember. A 1 means they didn't remember very much, and a 4 means they remembered at least three good things in a logical order while giving the main idea. K-Hesitations-These are words that the student struggled on but still got right. L-This is how well they decoded. A 1 would mean that they had to sound out most words and a 4 means there were no issues at all. M-This shows how well they did with decoding multi-syllable words. N-This is how many mistakes they made using the short vowel sounds. Q-This is how many mistakes they made using the long vowel sounds.

Does a one-minute reading only tell us how many words a student read? Often that is the only reason we use it. However, we can use it for so much more. With closer examination, we can use the one-minute reading to check a number of important things. It is amazing how many things you can tell from a one-minute reading.

At this point, I want to give a general idea of how I track notes. You can do whatever works for you. If a word is mispronounced, I cross it out and write the word that is said above it. This way I can determine what kind of error it is. Examples include mispronunciations and substitutions. I circle the word if the student does not say anything in about three seconds. This lets me know if the word was pronounced to them. As stated earlier, do what works for you. The key is to make sure you track the words missed so that these words can be further analyzed.

I developed the One-Minute Reading Breakdown Chart (Form D) to make optimum use of the one-minute readings. Using this chart, we can look for patterns of errors along with tracking improvement. One really important thing to remember when using this chart is to just do the best you can while tracking errors. It will get easier to do this as time goes on. If you are not completely sure about what type of error it is, use your best instinct or guess. This chart has been extremely useful for me in planning interventions for my students. The following section will break down the chart components for you. Each column in the table is labeled with a letter. Match the letter with the description below. Again, keep in mind that the information in the tables doesn't have to be perfect. Do the best you can. You will become more accurate as time goes on. I do not want you to spend too much time analyzing an area and becoming frustrated. These terms are also included as a key on the bottom of the One-Minute Reading Breakdown Chart (Form D).

Components of this Chart

A-Total words: This is how many total correct words per minute that the student read.

B-Total errors: This is how many errors that the student read.

C-Sight word errors: This is the amount of errors made on words that don't sound out.

D-Fluency: On a scale of 1 to 4, how fluently does the student read? 1 is slow like a robot. 2 is okay, 3 is very good, and 4 is perfect (all words correct, sounds like they are talking in a normal conversation).

E-Problems chunking: These are the errors on words that sound out.

F-Mispronounced: These are words on which the student got the first sound(s) correct but missed the ending.

G-Substitutions: These are errors that the students made by saying a completely different word that doesn't sound out at all. Often the reader will say a word that might make sense with the meaning of the sentence, but is clearly not the word.

H-Pronounced to students: These are words that were not attempted. I usually give three seconds before I instruct the student to move on to the next word.

I-Do Mistakes change meaning? Does the error not make sense, but the student continues as if they don't notice.

J-Retelling: This is what they remember. A 1 means they didn't remember very much, and a 4 means they remembered at least three good things in a logical order while giving the main idea.

K-Hesitations but correct: With this, the reader pauses, thinks about it, and gets it correct.

L-Decoding skills: On a scale of 1 to 4, this is how well they decoded. A 1 would mean that they had to sound out most words and a 4 means there were no issues at all.

M- Multiple syllable words missed: This is the number of words missed that had more than one syllable. The first number is the total number missed and the second number is the total number of words containing more than one syllable.

N- Errors with short vowel sounds: Words missed that had short vowel sounds.

O-Errors with long vowel sounds: Words missed that had long vowel sounds. An example would be the student saying the word "bake" as "back."

Chapter Twelve

One-Minute Reading Breakdown Chart (Form E) - Example

(or "How much can a one-minute reading tell us about this student?")

Let's Take a Look!

Here we have a One-Minute Reading Breakdown Chart (Form E) of a second-grade student. We will call this student "Reid."

Figure 12.1

One Minute Reading Breakdown

	A total words	B total errors	C sight words errors (words that don't sound out)	D fluency (1-4)	E problems chunking (clarifying)- these are mistakes on words that sound out	F mispronounced (first sound right, but ending wrong)	G substitutions (completely different word-guess based on the words around it)	H pronounced to students (did not attempt orally)	I Do mistakes change meaning (is it the same part of speech or does it make sense?)	J retelling (1-4) How many important details were retold? 4 is the best	K hesitations but correct (struggled at first but got it)	L decoding skills (1-4)	M multi-syllable words	N Trouble with long vowel	O Trouble with short vowel
#1	34 WPM	1 err	1	2 of 4	0	0	1	1	yes	2 of 4	2	3 of 4	1 of 4	0	1
#2	36 WPM	2 err	1	2 of 4	0	1	0	1	yes	2 of 4	2	3 of 4	0 of 4	0	2
#3	43 WPM	2 err	0	2.25 of 4	2	1	0	1	yes	2 of 4	1	3 of 4	1 of 6	0	2
#4	48 WPM	1 err	0	2.5 of 4	1	0	0	1	-	3 of 4	1	3 of 4	1 of 7	0	1
#5	52 WPM	1 err	1	2.75 of 4	0	1	0	0	yes	3 of 4	1	3.25 of 4	1 of 7	0	0
#6	49 WPM	2 err	0	2.75 of 4	2	2	0	0	yes	3 of 4	1	3 of 4	1 of 7	1	1
#7	52 WPM	1 err	0	2.75 of 4	1	1	0	1	yes	3 of 4	1	3 of 4	0 of 8	0	1
#8	55 WPM	2 err	1	2.5 of 4	1	0	0	2	yes	3 of 4	3	2.75 of 4	1 of 8	1	1
#9	55 WPM	2 err	1	2.5 of 4	1	2	0	0	yes	3 of 4	1	3 of 4	2 of 8	1	1
#10	54 WPM	2 err	1	2.5 of 4	2	0	0	2	-	3 of 4	1	2.75 of 4	1 of 9	0	0
#11	61 WPM	3 err	1	2.5 of 4	2	0	1	2	no	3 of 4	1	2.75 of 4	3 of 6	1	1
#12	67 WPM	0 err	0	2.75 of 4	0	0	0	0	-	4 of 4	0	3.75 of 4	0 of 10	0	0
#13	73 WPM	1 err	0	3 of 4	1	0	0	1	-	4 of 4	0	3.5 of 4	0 of 10	0	1
#14	64 WPM	1 err	0	2.5 of 4	1	0	0	1	-	4 of 4	0	3 of 4	0 of 12	0	1
#15	64 WPM	1 err	0	2.5 of 4	1	1	0	0	-	4 of 4	0	3.5 of 4	0 of 9	0	1
#16	70 WPM	0 err	0	2.75 of 4	0	0	0	0	-	3 of 4	1	4 of 4	0 of 9	0	0
#17	70 WPM	0 err	0	2.75 of 4	0	0	0	0	-	4 of 4	0	4 of 4	0 of 12	0	0
fluency		accuracy	word recognition and fluency	fluency	decoding	decoding	decoding	decoding	comprehension go/context clues	comprehension	decoding and fluency	decoding and fluency	decoding and fluency	decoding	decoding

What do the different columns mean?

A-This is words per minute. We want to see this number go up. The goal for first grade at the end of the year is 47. B-Errors-This is total mistakes. We want to see this go down. Even just one or two is an improvement. This is also called accuracy. C-Sight words-These are words that don't sound out, like "the". If the number is high, you can practice the sight word lists. D -This is fluency (accuracy, speed, and tone of voice). A 1 is like a robot and a 4 is just like you are talking. E-Chunking-These are missed words that the student should know how to clarify if given time. F-Mispronounced. These mistakes usually involve the student looking at the first letter and guessing. G-Substitutions-These mistakes usually mean that the student guessed what would be next without really looking. H- With these errors, the students were given about three seconds and couldn't make a guess, so they were told the word. I- A mistake that "changes meaning" is a mistake that doesn't make sense, but the student continues on. J-This is what they remember. A 1 means they didn't remember very much, and a 4 means they remembered at least three good things in a logical order while giving the main idea. K-Hesitations-These are words that the student struggled on but still got right. A 1 would mean that they had to sound out most words and a 4 means there were no issues at all. L-This is how well they did with decoding multi-syllable words. M-This shows how well they decoded. A 1 means they struggled on but still got right. N-This is how many mistakes they made using the short vowel sounds. O-This is how many mistakes they made using the long vowel sounds.

Let's Take a Look!

As stated earlier, our goal is to carefully look at the passage and look for patterns of errors. Some of the errors we will look at we also examined in other charts. An example of this would be WPM. However, I felt it important to include this chart because I want this to be a "big picture" chart.

WPM (Column A)

When we look at this student's WPM scores (Column A), we notice the scores constantly going up. This is a good sign, but we still know little about other issues that might be going on. That is where this chart is useful. Let's dig deeper.

Errors (Column B)

Next we will check the error column (Column B). A student might get a high word-per-minute score but still make many errors. This could have a huge effect on comprehension. If there is a problem with errors, we need to be aware of it so we can take proper action. The key to this is to see if a student's accuracy is getting better. Reid's last two progress monitoring showed no errors. Even before that, her error count was low. Knowing this, I feel pretty confident about Reid's ability to read for accuracy.

Sight Word Errors (Column C)

The next column is sight word errors (Column C). These words do not sound out. If the word contains a digraph that the students have worked on and should know, I usually do not count them as a sight word. I often think of these words as being words that a student would use with flashcards. Reid does not miss many sight words. This seems to be a fairly consistent pattern. That would suggest to me that she has a pretty good grasp of sight words.

Fluency (Column D)

Next is fluency (Column D). Fluency is the ability to read a text accurately, quickly, and with expression. It is important to take all three of these details into consideration when determining fluency. If a student's fluency is at a high level, their comprehension is usually at a higher level. This is due to the fact that they have more attention to devote to understanding what is read. As stated previously, I use a scale of 1 to 4 to rate fluency. As we look over this student's fluency, she has been improving. However, her scores suggest that she still needs fluency practice. A 2.75 is adequate, but we really want to aim for a 4. Repeated reading would be a good intervention to use.

Chunking Errors (Column E)

The first one of which is her success with chunking (Column E). These are words missed that sound out. Reid did have some trouble chunking at the beginning of the year but nothing that should have set off too many alarms. Her chunking errors have remained low throughout the year. What does concern me is that her chunking errors (and errors overall) are very low but her fluency score is still not as high as I want. I see this as more evidence that extra fluency intervention should help her.

Mispronounced (Column F)

The next column is words mispronounced (Column F). I count these as words where the first sound was pronounced right, but the ending was wrong. This could suggest that the student needs help with word endings or they are being careless and just making a guess based on the first letter. What if this section shows the student is struggling in this error? If this is the case, we can carefully listen when they are orally reading to see if we can get a better idea of whether they are just hurrying or really do have decoding issues.

Substitutions (Column G)

The next thing we will look at is substitutions (Column G). Substitutions are errors that happen when the reader says a completely different word in place of the actual word. Often these words are the reader's best guess based on the words around it. This area does not seem to be a problem for this student. If it was a problem, one plan could be to slow her down.

Pronounced to Student (Column H)

Let's now look at the column marked "pronounced to student" (Column H). I mark this category when I have to pronounce the word to a student. Typically, I wait three seconds before pronouncing it. This number is usually pretty high for a struggling young reader. A high number here suggests that the student does not have sufficient decoding skills. This would mean some basic phonics decoding interventions are needed. Reid does not have any noticeable problems in this area.

Does the Mistake Change Meaning? (Column I)

The next column is "Does mistake change meaning?" (Column I). For this I focus on the error. I look to see if it makes sense. If the word does not make sense and the student does not pause or indicate that it doesn't sound right, I will count it in this category. I like to know this type of error because it is an indication of comprehension. We need to be aware if our students are realizing their mistakes. In this case, Reid has not made any errors for the last few times she was progress monitored. Therefore, we won't worry about this too much. However, at the beginning of the year she had problems with not indicating that she knew something didn't make sense. I helped her with this by encouraging her to slow down after each sentence and think about if the sentence made sense. Gradually she became better at noticing her mistakes. When this happened, I backed off from having her pause after each sentence.

Fluency (Column J)

Let's look at Column J—fluency. We will be using the fluency scale again here. Reid has done a good job with her fluency. She has consistently scored a 3 or a 4 in the past several weeks. Next, I consider if I feel that her retelling carries over to other works. Going from my experience working with her, I would say that it does.

Hesitations (Column K)

Next, is "hesitations" in Column K. I count hesitations as words that are not clarified right away but are eventually properly decoded. She has had no or few hesitations. This is not an issue because we know from earlier that she makes very few overall errors.

Decoding Skills (Column L)

Then we have "decoding skills" in Column L. Again I use a scale of 1 to 4. This is objective; you can use your best judgement. A 1 is sounding out sound by sound with several errors. A 2 is sounding out some words or making a few mistakes. A 3 is good with words read as a whole with just a mistake or two. A 4 is perfect with no mistakes. When we take a look at Reid's scores, we see that she is doing well with decoding. There are no concerns here.

Multisyllable Words Missed (Column M)

Column M is how many multisyllable words were missed. The first number is total errors and the second number is how many multisyllable words the reader attempted. This knowledge is useful because it allows us to decide if we should focus on breaking words into syllables or parts if the reader has many errors in this category. Reid is doing well in this area.

Short Vowel Errors (Column N)

Column N is how many mistakes were made with words containing short vowel sounds. This is useful because if we see a lot of errors here, we know to go back and focus on practicing the short vowel sounds. Since Reid is not making many errors over, this is not an issue.

Long Vowel Errors (Column O)

Column O is similar but instead of short vowels, we look at errors with words containing long vowels. Again, it helps us focus our instruction if we see continuous errors with one type of word. Don't overthink what category a word might go into if it is irregular. Our data does not need to be perfect. We need to be as close as we can but we don't want to stress out while filling out these charts. Since Reid is not making many errors over, this is not an issue.

Chapter Thirteen
Overview of Progress Monitoring (Form F)

(Or, "Okay, now what do we do?")

Overview of Progress Monitoring

The last thing we will look at is a summary sheet that I use for parent meetings. The first thing I kept in mind when I was creating this sheet was that I wanted something to present the information to the parents in a simple way. This sheet is also used to provide suggestions for interventions that parents can use at home. There is a blank copy with room for more comments at the back of this book. You can also find an electronic copy you can adjust at www.foustreading.simplesite.com.

Overview of Progress Monitoring

NOTES ON DECODING

How are decoding skills?   Struggling   OK   Does Well

Is there usually a pattern of mistakes?   Yes   No
If so, what?

Do they attempt words that they don't know?

Do they usually notice mistakes?

How is sight word recognition?

If extra practice is needed, what do I recommend?

NOTES ON FLUENCY (Speed, accuracy, and phrasing)
How is fluency?

If fluency is an issue, is their decoding at a high enough level to focus on fluency practice?

What would I recommend for fluency if needed?

NOTES ON COMPREHENSION
How is their retelling?

Does this reflect their use of comprehension skills?

What would I recommend?

Chapter Fourteen

Overview of Progress Monitoring (Form F) - Example

(Or "What did we find out and what can be done to help our student improve?")

Checking Our Data

For this chapter, we are going to take a look at the data of a student we will call "Skyler." We will look at Skyler's forms. These forms are:

Progress Monitoring Student Report (Form A)

Nonsense Word Table (Form B)

Fluency Chart (Form C)

Retell Chart (Form D)

One-Minute Reading Breakdown Chart (Form E)

After this, I will create an Overview of Progress Monitoring (Form F) for Skyler.

First Grade Title Progress Report (Form A)

DIBELS Results-January *(* means winter benchmark met)*

NWF (nonsense word fluency) 43/8-benchmark	ORF 23-benchmark	Retell n/a	Accuracy 78%	Composite 130-benchmark
89*/26*	39 WPM*	12/1	91%	234*

DIBELS Results-September *(underlined if benchmark was met)*

LNF (letter naming fluency) No benchmark	PSF (phoneme segmentation fluency) 40-benchmark	NWF (nonsense word fluency) 27/1-benchmark	Composite 113-benchmark
35 letters	67	23/3	125

STAR and SEL *(Key: urg.=needs extra intervention , int.=needs intervention, OW=on watch (may need intervention), at=at or above benchmark)*

	STAR (SS, GE & IRL)	SEL
#1	55-int., 0.2, PP	648-at
#2	77-at, 0.8, PP	752-at
#3	84-at, 1.1, PP	?

Progress Monitoring: *(underlined means first benchmark met, * Means 2nd met, ^ means 3rd met)*

	LNF	PSF (40)	NWF (58/13)	ORF (47 WPM)	Retell # (15)/qual (na)	Accuracy
#1	-	-	48/16	10 WPM	2/1	5 errors
#2	-	72	48/9	-	-	-
#3	-	-	68*/20*	18 WPM	6/1	8 errors
#4	-	-	70*/21	25 WPM*	5/1	5 errors
#5	-	-	75*/25*	33 WPM*	10/1	3 errors
#6	-	-	67*/20*	47 WPM*	10/1	5 errors
#7	-	-	82*/23*	35 WPM*	10/1	7 errors
#8	-	-	-	50 WPM^	13/1	3 errors

AR: *(as of 1/16/19)*

Total Points	%	Level
28.3 points	74.9%	1.9

Interventions Used: *Phonics Dance* (for decoding words with digraphs)/ *37 most common chunks* (for help with decoding and word recognition)/ *iPad apps that focus on decoding such as Starfall and Reading Magic/ Snap Words* (for rapid recognition of sight words)/ *Various decodable readers* (for decoding practice and fluency)

---

*Key: **NWF**-reading made-up words **ORF**-oral reading fluency (how many words read in a minute) **Composite**-a combination score of all the areas **Retell # and quality**-how many words and how many details—4 is best for quality **STAR and SEL**-these are exams that test comprehension and other skills **GE**-grade equivalent—what level they tested **IRL**-instructional reading level, the level that they should read at to improve (not too easy and not too hard)*

(Form B)

	1	2	3	4	5	6	7	8	9	10	11	12	13	14	15	16	17	18	19	20
CLS	48	48	68	70	75	67	82													
WRC	16	9	20	21	25	20	23													
Total mis.	2	6	3	6	2	4	8													
Fluency ind. sounds																				
Fluency whole words	x	x	x	x	x	x	x													
a																				
b	1	3	2	3	1	2	1													
c																				
d		2					1													
e							3													
f																				
g		2																		
h																				
i						1	1													
j																				
k																				
l																				
m																				
n						1														
o	1		1	1	1		1													
p				1		1														
q																				
r																				
s																				
t																				
u																				
v																				
w																				
x																				
y				1																
z																				

Name: Skyler

(Form C)

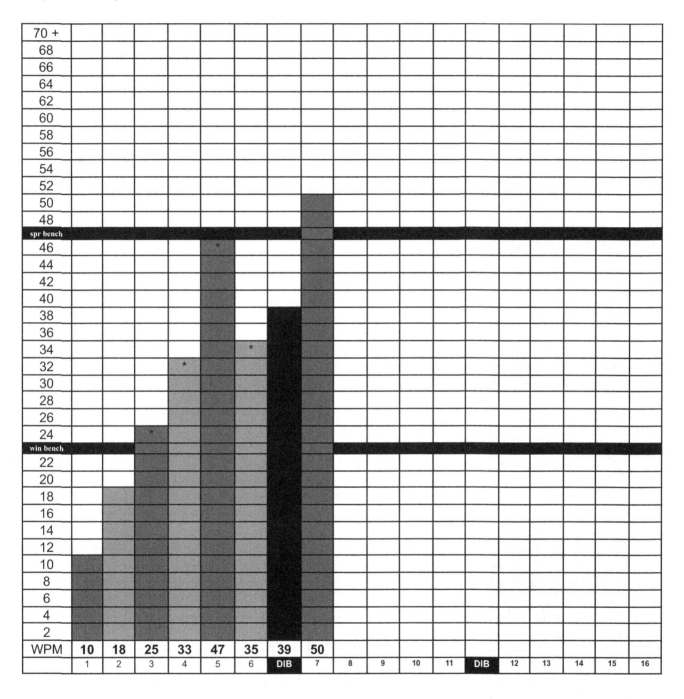

WPM	10	18	25	33	47	35	39	50									
	1	2	3	4	5	6	DIB	7	8	9	10	11	DIB	12	13	14	15	16

*means they had an odd number of words per minute, so add one word to the total. Example, if the bar goes up to 20 and there is a *, the total is 21. The first bold line is the winter benchmark and the second one is the spring benchmark.

Name: Skyler

(Form D)

	Score	Very few details	3 or more details	3 or more details in order	3 or more details in order which also tell the main idea
DIBELS	1 of 4				
Progress Monitoring #1	1 of 4				
Progress Monitoring #2	1 of 4				
Progress Monitoring #3	1 of 4				
Progress Monitoring #4	1 of 4				
Progress Monitoring #5	1 of 4				
Progress Monitoring #6	1 of 4				
Progress Monitoring #7	1 of 4				
Progress Monitoring #8	1 of 4				
Progress Monitoring #9	1 of 4				
Progress Monitoring #10	1 of 4				
Progress Monitoring #11	1 of 4				
Progress Monitoring #12	1 of 4				
Progress Monitoring #13	1 of 4				
Progress Monitoring #14	1 of 4				
Progress Monitoring #15	1 of 4				
Progress Monitoring #16	1 of 4				
Progress Monitoring #17	1 of 4				
Progress Monitoring #18	1 of 4				
Progress Monitoring #19	1 of 4				
Progress Monitoring #20	1 of 4				

Name: Skyler

(Form E)

One Minute Reading Breakdown

	A	B	C	D	E	F	G	H	I	J	K	L	M	N	O
	total words	total errors	sight words errors (words that don't sound out)	fluency (1-4)	problems chunking (first sound right, but ending wrong)	mispronounced (completely different word, guessed word, based on words around it)	substitutions	pronounced to students (did not attempt orally)	Do mistakes change meaning? (Is it the same part of speech or does it make sense)	retelling (1-4) How many important details were recalled? 4 is the best	hesitations, but correct (struggled at first but got it)	decoding skills (1-4) overall decode/chunk/sound out? How good were their decoding skills? 4 is the best	multi-syllable words (How many words with more than one vowel did they miss?)	trouble with short vowel sounds (How many short vowel words did they miss?)	trouble with long vowel sounds (How many long vowel words did they miss?)
				out of 4						out of 4		out of 4			
#1	10 WPM	5 err	2	1 of 4	3	1	0	4	yes	1 of 4	1	1 of 4	3 of 4	1	3
#2	18 WPM	8 err	2	1.5 of 4	6	7	1	0	yes	1 of 4	1	1.25 of 4	3 of 6	1	3
#3	25 WPM	5 err	2	2.5 of 4	3	5	0	0	yes	1 of 4	2	2 of 4	0 of 3	1	1
#4	33 WPM	3 err	0	3 of 4	3	2	0	1	yes	1 of 4	4	2.5 of 4	1 of 1	2	1
#5	47 WPM	5 err	1	3 of 4	4	5	0	0	yes	2 of 4	5	2.5 of 4	1 of 4	0	3
#6	35 WPM	7 err	0	2.5 of 4	7	7	0	0	yes	1 of 4	7	2.25 of 4	1 of 4	1	5
#7	50 WPM	3 err	0	3 of 4	3	0	0	0	yes	0 of 4	3	2.75 of 4	0 of 3	0	2
	fluency	accuracy	word recognition and fluency	fluency	decoding	decoding	decoding	decoding	comprehension/context clues	comprehension	decoding and fluency	decoding and fluency	decoding and fluency	decoding	decoding

What do the different columns mean?

A-This is words per minute. We want to see this number go up. The goal for first grade at the end of the year is 47. **B**-Errors-This is total mistakes. We want to see this number go down. Even just one or two is an improvement. This is also called accuracy. **C**-sight words-These are words that don't sound out like "the". If the number is high, you can practice the sight word lists. **D**- This is fluency (accuracy, speed, and tone of voice) A "1" is like a robot and a "4" is just like you are talking. **E**-Chunking-These are missed words that the student should know how to clarify if given time. **F**-Mispronounced. These mistakes usually involve the student looking at the first letter and guessing. **G**- Substitutions-These mistakes usually mean that the student guessed what would be next without really looking. **H**- With these errors, the students were given about 3 seconds and couldn't make a guess so they were told the word. **I**- A mistake that 'changes meaning' is a mistake that doesn't make sense but they continue on. **J**- This is what they remember. A "1" means they didn't remember very much, and a "4" means they remembered at least 3 good things in a logical order while giving the main idea. **K**-Hesitations- These are words that they struggled on but still got right. **L**- This is how well they decoded. A "1" would mean that they had to sound out most words and a "4" means there were no issues at all. **M**- This shows how well they did with decoding multi-syllable words. **N**- This is how many mistakes they made using the short vowel sounds. **O**- This is how many mistakes they made using the long vowel sounds.

Completing an Overview (Form F):

Now, let's remind ourselves what a blank Overview of Progress Monitoring (Form F) looks like.

Figure 14.1

Overview of Progress Monitoring

NOTES ON DECODING

How are decoding skills?   Struggling   OK   Does Well

Is there usually a pattern of mistakes?   Yes   No
If so, what?

Do they attempt words they don't know?

Do they usually notice mistakes?

How is sight word recognition?

If extra practice is needed, what do I recommend?

NOTES ON FLUENCY: (Speed, accuracy, and phrasing)

How is fluency?

If fluency is an issue, is their decoding at a high enough level to focus on fluency practice?

What I would recommend for fluency if needed?

NOTES ON COMPREHENSION

How is their retelling?

Does this reflect their use of comprehension skills?

What I would recommend?

Let's go through the questions on the Overview of Progress Monitoring (Form E) one at a time. We will start with the "Notes on Decoding" section.

"How are the student's decoding skills?"

For this question, let's focus on two forms—the Progress Report (A) and the Nonsense Word Chart (B).

For the Progress Report (A), let's focus in on the NWF. (figure 14.2)

Figure 14.2

NWF (58/13)
48/16
48/9
68*/20*
70*/21
75*/25*
67*/20*
82*/23*

We can see that the latest benchmark was 58 total sounds and 13 complete words. Our student did his last check at 82 total sounds and 23 complete words. If we check the weeks leading into this, we see similar results. This is a great sign that he is doing well in decoding. However, let's check one more thing. Let's look at his Nonsense Word Chart (B). We will focus in on mistakes made (14.3).

Figure 14.3

Total Mistakes Made
2
6
3
6
2
4
8

These numbers are concerning, even though his NWF score is high. He has been making a lot of errors. This is something that could have been overlooked with Form B. Looking at the letters he missed, we see the pattern of missing "b," "d," "e," "i," and "o." This shows me he needs to practice differentiating between "d" and "b" and also to focus on vowels. So I would write something like the following sentence to answer the question: *"His overall decoding is typically good and fairly fast. However, he can get careless and struggles with the vowels."*

Let's take a look at the next question under the "Notes on Decoding" section.

"Is there usually a pattern of mistakes? Yes/No"
"If so, what?"

For this we will focus on the Nonsense Word Chart (B).

As we noted earlier, the student had trouble with the vowels and "b" and "d." I would write something like the following to answer the question: *"Yes. I have noticed that he often confuses "b" and "d" and also struggles with the vowels."*

Let's look at the next question under "decoding."

"Do they attempt words that they don't know?"

For this we will focus on some information from the One-Minute Breakdown Form (E). Because we are trying to get a good idea if the reader tries words they don't know, or if they are intimidated by unknown words, we will look at how many words are pronounced to them.

Figure 14.4

Pronounced to Students (did not attempt orally)
4
0
0
1
0
0
0

This chart tells us that he has not had any real issues with this since the beginning of the year. I would write something like the following to answer the question: *"Yes, he usually makes good guesses for words that he does not know."*

Now let's look at the next question under "Decoding."

"Does he usually notice mistakes?"

For this we will focus on some information from the One-Minute Breakdown (Form E). Because we are checking to see if the student notices mistakes, we will check to see if his mistakes change meaning. If he stopped and expressed confusion at his mistakes, I put "yes."

Figure 14.5

Do mistakes change meaning? (Is it the same part of speech or does it make sense?)
yes

83

yes
yes
yes
yes
yes
yes
yes
yes
yes
yes
yes

All the "yeses" suggest that he does not notice the mistakes or would rather just keep reading instead of stopping. I would write something like this to answer the question: *"No, he usually keeps reading. If he does notice, he will often just move on without trying to sound it out."*

Let's look at the next question on the "Decoding" section.

"If extra practice is needed, what do I recommend?"

For this, I would reflect on what I previously noted about decoding. I would give the reader some flashcards with nonsense words containing all the vowel sounds. I would have the parent work slowly with these cards while the student takes note of the vowel first. I may also give copies of decodable stories and encourage the student to read them carefully.

"How is sight word recognition?"

For this I will take a look at the "sight words" column on the "One-Minute Breakdown Form" (E).

Figure 14.6

Sight Words Errors (words that don't sound out)
2
2
2
0
1
0
0
0
1
0
2
0

Looking at this, I don't see much to be worried about. The passages that I use for the one-minute readings contain several level-appropriate sight words. With this in mind, I note that he hasn't made many mistakes on these words. I would write something like this to answer the question: *"He has been doing a good job on recognizing sight words."*

Let's look at the final question under the "Decoding" section.

"If extra practice is needed, what do I recommend?"

For this, I would reflect on what I had previously noted about decoding. I would give the student some flashcards with nonsense words containing all the vowel sounds. I would have the parent work slowly with these cards while the student takes note of the vowel first. I may also give copies of decodable stories and encourage the student to read them carefully.

Next we will look at the "Notes on Fluency" section.

"How is fluency?"

Let's look at the information included on Fluency Graph (C) and the One-Minute Breakdown Form (E). Both of these forms have information on them that will give you a good idea of fluency level.

Figure 14.7

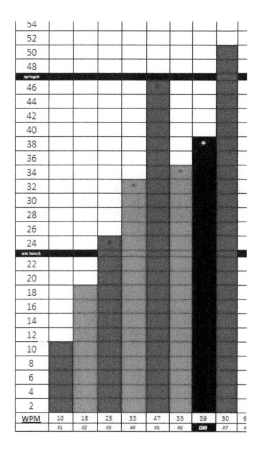

This graph is from "Fluency Graph (Form C)." The solid black line is the winter DIBELS WPM benchmark. At first glance, the progress is very promising. We see an improvement over time, and the student is already at the spring benchmark. This is great, however we need to check some other things. Fluency is more than just words per minute. It also includes accuracy and tone of voice. For this, let's look at a couple of columns from the "One-Minute Breakdown Form."

Let's look at total errors first.

Figure 14.8

Total Errors
5 err
8 err
5 err
3 err
5 err
7 err
3 err

His error count is still pretty high, but is improving.

Now let's look at his fluency rating from the same chart.

Figure 14.9

Fluency (1-4)
out of 4
1 of 4
1.5 of 4
2.5 of 4
3 of 4
3 of 4
2.5 of 4
3 of 4

Quick Review of Fluency Scale

1. Slow, like a robot. Sounds out words.
2. Okay, but still a little slow. May sound out a word or two.
3. Pretty good.
4. Perfect! Sounds like the student is talking. Not too fast and not too slow. Reads with expression.

I would write something like the following to answer the question: *"His fluency is good at this point. He still makes some errors, but his tone is coming along nicely."*

Let's look at the next question under the "Fluency" section.

"If fluency is an issue, is his decoding at a high enough level to focus on fluency practice?"

For this, I would write something like this: *"His decoding is sufficient and we will keep working on fluency so he keeps improving."*

Let's look at the next question under the "Fluency" section.

"What would I recommend for fluency if needed?"

For this, I would write something like the following: *"I would recommend taking a page from the book he is reading and read it several times, then give him a score or a scale of 1 to 4 with four being the best. I would also give him a paper with the scale on it."*

Now let's take a look at the "Notes on Comprehension" section.

"How is his retelling?"

For this question, I will focus on the retell column (fig. 14.10) of his "Progress Monitoring Student Report" (Form A).

Figure 14.10

Retell # (15)/qual (na)
2/1
-
6/1
5/1
10/1
10/1
10/1
13/1

To quickly review, the first number is the total number of words recalled. This number gives us good information, but I feel the second number is more important. The second number is the quality of the retell. A 1 is poor quality, a 2 is two details, a 3 is three details, and a 4 is three or more details told in a way that conveys the main idea.

We can see that while his total number of words is improving, the total number is still below the current benchmark. Even more importantly, we see that the quality is a 1 and hasn't been higher than that.

For this question, I would write something like the following: *"Data shows me that, while he is retelling some of the story, he often misses many important facts. This could be due to focusing more on getting the words correct than what they mean."*

Let's look at the next question under the "Notes on Comprehension" section.

"Does this reflect their use of comprehension skills?"

For this, I would write something like the following: *"Yes, I feel at this point they are more worried about getting the words read quickly. However, this is something that can be improved."*

What would I recommend?

Because we need him to slow down, I would suggest something like the following: *"I would have him stop and ask "who," "what," "where," "when," and "why" questions after every page. If it is a nonfiction book, I want him to use the Nonfiction Chart, and if it is a fiction book, I want him to use a story map or similar graphic organizer."* (These are included in the back of the book.)

Let's look at the completed Overview of Progress Monitoring Form on the following page.

Overview of Progress Monitoring

NOTES ON DECODING

How are the student's decoding skills? *His overall decoding is typically good and fairly fast. However, he can get careless and struggles with the vowels.*

Is there usually a pattern of mistakes?   **Yes**   No
If so, what? *Yes. I have noticed that he often confuses "b" and "d" and also struggles with the vowels.*

Does he attempt words that he doesn't know? *Yes, he usually makes good guesses for words that he does not know.*

Does he usually notice mistakes? *No, he keeps reading. If he does notice, he will often just move on without trying to sound it out.*

If extra practice is needed, what do I recommend? *Practice the flashcards while making sure he is focusing on the vowels.*

NOTES ON SIGHT WORDS

How is sight word recognition? *He has been doing a good job on recognizing sight words.*

If extra practice is needed, what do I recommend? *As of now, he is doing a nice job on the sight words. However, we will keep a close eye on this as we add more difficult sight words.*

NOTES ON FLUENCY: (Speed, accuracy, and phrasing)

How is fluency? *His fluency is good at this point. He still makes some errors, but his tone is coming along nicely.*

If fluency is an issue, is his decoding at a high enough level to focus on fluency practice? *His decoding is sufficient and we will keep working on fluency so he keeps improving.*

What would I recommend for fluency if needed? *I would recommend taking a page from the book he is reading and read it several times, then give him a score or a scale of 1 to 4 with four being the best. I would also give him a paper with the scale on it.*

NOTES ON COMPREHENSION

How is their retelling? *Data shows me that, while they are retelling some of the story, they often miss many important facts. This could be due to focusing more on getting the words correct than what they mean.*

Does this reflect their use of comprehension skills? *Yes, I feel at this point they are more worried about getting the words read quickly. However, this is something that can be improved.*

What would I recommend? *Since we need him to slow down, I would suggest something like the following: I would have him stop and ask "who," "what," "where," "when," and "why" questions after every page. If it is a nonfiction book, I want him to use the Nonfiction Chart, and if it is a fiction book, I want him to use a story map or similar graphic organizer.*

Chapter Fifteen
Final Thoughts

(or "What now?")

In the first chapter, I wrote a list of things I wanted you to keep in mind. Let's review these points.

- I do not want this book to be overwhelming.

- Remember that these forms can be adapted.

- You do not need to use this with everyone.

- The data doesn't have to be perfect.

- You can either hand write these forms or type them.

- It's not just about data tracking.

- This can be used in most elementary grade levels.

- I like to keep things simple.

Please keep these things in mind as you think about what might be helpful to you. Select a student who is struggling. Ask yourself if you have kept consistent data on the student. If not, that is okay. Pick a day of the week to progress monitor this student. Start with a one-minute reading. Administer it, and do your best to fill out the charts I've discussed here. You may even make changes to these charts that will benefit you. After you become comfortable with one student, you can add another. Do what works for you.

Remember to consult your data on a regular basis. Ask yourself if you see positive improvements. Show your charts to your students. Help them feel proud about their accomplishments. You will be able to find something that works for you and will help you get the most out of your time.

References

McLaughlin, M., & Fisher, L. (2005). Practical Fluency. (1st ed.). New York, NY: Scholastic.

National Institute of Child Health and Human Development (2000). Report of the National Reading Panel. Teaching children to read: An evidence-based assessment of the scientific research literature on reading and its implications for reading instruction (NIH Publication No. 00-4769). Washington, DC: U.S. Government Printing Office.

Samuels, S. J. (1979). The method of repeated readings. The Reading Teacher, 32, 403- 408.

U.S. Department of Education, Institute of Education Sciences, National Center for Education Statistics, National Assessment of Educational Progress (NAEP), 2002 Oral ReadingStudy.

Wylie, R., & Durrell, D. (1970). Teaching vowels through phonograms. Elementary English, Vol. 47, 787-791.

APPENDIX 1—Progress Monitoring Charts

In this section, I have included several charts to use for progress monitoring. There is a description for each one. Some are more detailed and specifically use certain assessments. Others are more general. You will find templates you can adjust for your own needs at **www.foustreading.simplesite.com**.

The graph on the following page is used for first grade. This is to be in conjunction with DIBELS, STAR Testing, and Accelerated Reader. If a section does not apply to you, simply skip it. You may also make changes to the template at **www.foustreading.simplesite.com.**

Progress Monitoring Student Report *(Form A)*

DIBELS Results-Spring *(* means spring benchmark met)*

NWF (nonsense word fluency) 43/8-benchmark	ORF 23-benchmark	Retell n/a	Accuracy 78%	Composite 130-benchmark

DIBELS Results-Winter *(* means winter benchmark met)*

NWF (nonsense word fluency) 43/8-benchmark	ORF 23-benchmark	Retell n/a	Accuracy 78%	Composite 130-benchmark

DIBELS Results-Fall *(underlined if benchmark was met)*

LNF (letter naming fluency)	PSF (phoneme segmentation fluency)	NWF (nonsense word fluency)	Composite
No benchmark	40-benchmark	27/1-benchmark	113

STAR and SEL *(Key: urg.=needs extra intervention , int.=needs intervention, OW=on watch (may need ntervention), at=at or above benchmark)*

	STAR (SS, GE & IRL)	SEL	Baseline (Total and alt. baseline)
#1			
#2			
#3			
#4			

Results of Progress Monitoring: *(underlined means first benchmark met, * Means second met, numbers in () indicate difference from last DIB)*

	LNF	PSF (40)	NWF (43/8)	ORF (23)	Retell (# and quality)	Accuracy
#1						
#2						
#3						
#4						
#5						
#6						
#7						
#8						
#9						
#10						

AR:

Total Points	%	Level

Interventions Used:

The graph on the following page is used for second grade. This is to be used with DIBELS, STAR Testing, and Accelerated Reader. You may also make changes to the template at **www.foustreading.simplesite.com.**

Progress Monitoring Student Report *(Form A)*

DIBELS-April *(^ if benchmark was met)*

ORF	Accuracy	Retell & Quality	Composite
87 WPM-benchmark	97%-benchmark	27-benchmark	238-benchmark

DIBELS Results-January *(* if winter benchmark was met)*

ORF	Accuracy	Retell/qual	Composite
72-benchmark	96%-benchmark	21/2-benchmark	190-benchmark

DIBELS Results-September *(underlined if benchmark was met)*

NWF (54/13)	ORF (52)	Accuracy (90%)	Retell/quality (16/2)	Composite (141)

STAR/Baseline *(Key: urg.=needs extra intervention , int.=needs intervention, OW=on watch (may need intervention), at=at or above benchmark)*

	STAR (SS, GE & IRL)
#1	
#2	
#3	
#4	
#5	

Progress Monitoring: *(underlined means first benchmark met, * Means 2nd met, ^ means 3rd met)*

	NWF	ORF	Retell/qual	Accuracy
#1				
#2				
#3				
#4				
#5				
#6				
#7				
#8				
#9				
#10				
#11				

AR:

Total Points	%	Level

The graph on the following page is used for tracking one-minute progress monitoring of nonsense words and fluency passages. This is a more general form you can use for many types of assessments. You can make changes to the template at **www.foustreading.simplesite.com.**

Name:

Progress Monitoring Student Report

	NWF	ORF	Retell/qual	Accuracy
#1				
#2				
#3				
#4				
#5				
#6				
#7				
#8				
#9				
#10				
#11				
#12				
#13				
#14				
#15				
#16				
#17				
#18				
#19				
#20				

The Nonsense Word Chart (Form B) on the next page is used for tracking one-minute progress monitoring of nonsense words. This chart was described in detail in chapters 5 and 6. It is used to pinpoint exactly what letters the students are struggling with. You may also make changes to the template at **www.foustreading.simplesite.com.**

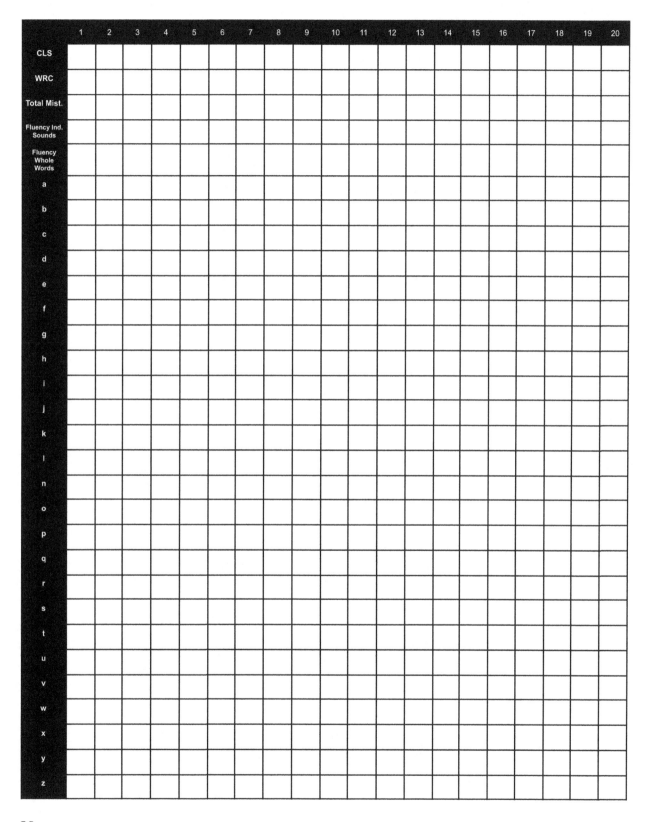

	1	2	3	4	5	6	7	8	9	10	11	12	13	14	15	16	17	18	19	20
CLS																				
WRC																				
Total Mist.																				
Fluency Ind. Sounds																				
Fluency Whole Words																				
a																				
b																				
c																				
d																				
e																				
f																				
g																				
h																				
i																				
j																				
k																				
l																				
n																				
o																				
p																				
q																				
r																				
s																				
t																				
u																				
v																				
w																				
x																				
y																				
z																				

Name:

The Fluency Chart (Form C) on this page is used for tracking words per minute on the one-minute readings. I use this one for first grade. This chart was described in detail in chapters 7 and 8. Besides tracking the data, it is very good for showing students to help motivate them to reach goals. You may also make changes to the template at **www.foustreading.simplesite.com.**

WPM																	
70																	
68																	
66																	
64																	
62																	
60																	
58																	
56																	
54																	
52																	
50																	
48																	
46																	
44																	
42																	
40																	
38																	
36																	
34																	
32																	
30																	
28																	
26																	
24																	
20																	
18																	
16																	
14																	
12																	
10																	
8																	
6																	
4																	
2																	
WPM																	
	1	2	3	4	5	6	7	8	9	10	11	12	13	14	15	16	17	18

*means they had an odd number of words per minute, so add one word to the total. Example, if the bar goes up to 20 and there is a *, the total is 21. The first bold line is the winter benchmark and the second one is the spring benchmark.

Name:

The Fluency Chart (Form C) on the next page is used for tracking words per minute on the one-minute readings. I use this one for second grade. This chart was described in detail in chapters 7 and 8. Besides tracking the data, it is very good for showing students to help motivate them to reach goals. You may also make changes to the template at **www.foustreading.simplesite.com.**

Name:

WPM	#1	#2	#3	#4	#5	#6	#7	#8	#9	#10	#11	#12	#13	#14	#15	#16	#17	#18	#19
80																			
78																			
76																			
74																			
72																			
70																			
68																			
66																			
64																			
62																			
60																			
58																			
56																			
54																			
52																			
50																			
48																			
46																			
44																			
42																			
40																			
38																			
36																			
34																			
32																			
30																			
28																			
26																			
24																			
22																			
20																			
18																			
16																			
14																			
Errors																			

* means to add one-for example, if the bar goes up to 30 and there is a *, the total would be 31 WPM

The Retell Chart (Form D) on the following page is used for the weekly retell scores. This chart was described in detail in Chapters 9 and 10. This chart is good for helping students realize there is more to reading than just reading quickly. You may also make changes to the template at **www.foustreading.simplesite.com.**

Retelling

	Score	Very few details	3 or more details	3 or more details in order	3 or more details in order which also tell the main idea
DIBELS					
Progress Monitoring #1					
Progress Monitoring #2					
Progress Monitoring #3					
Progress Monitoring #4					
Progress Monitoring #5					
Progress Monitoring #6					
Progress Monitoring #7					
Progress Monitoring #8					
Progress Monitoring #9					
Progress Monitoring #10					
Progress Monitoring #11					
Progress Monitoring #12					
Progress Monitoring #13					
Progress Monitoring #14					
Progress Monitoring #15					

Name_____

The One-Minute Reading Breakdown Chart (Form E) on the next page is used for tracking several different areas of a one-minute progress monitoring passage. This chart was described in detail in chapters 11 and 12. The purpose of this form is to pinpoint what kind of errors the student is making. This way, you can plan intervention to improve these types of errors. You may also make changes to the template at **www.foustreading.simplesite.com.**

One Minute Reading Breakdown

	A	B	C	D	E	F	G	H	I	J	K	L	M	N	O
	total words	total errors	sight words errors. (clarifying)- these are words that don't sound out)	fluency (1-4)	problems chunking	mispronounced (first sound right, but ending wrong)	substitutions (completely different word, guessed based on the words around it)	pronounced to students (did not attempt orally)	Do mistakes change meaning? (Is it the same part of speech or does it make sense?)	retelling (1-4) How many details were retold? 4 is the best	hesitations, but correct (struggled at first but got it)	decoding skills (1-4) How well did they decode/chunk/sound out? How good were their decoding skills? 4 is the best	multi-syllable words (how many words with more than one syllable did they miss?)	trouble with short vowel sounds (how many short vowel words did they miss?)	Trouble with long vowel sounds (how many long vowel words did they miss?)
#1				out of 4						out of 4		out of 4			
#2															
#3															
#4															
#5															
#6															
#7															
#8															
#9															
#10															
#11															
	fluency	accuracy	word recognition and fluency	fluency	decoding	decoding	decoding	decoding	comprehension/context clues	comprehension	decoding and fluency	decoding and fluency	decoding and fluency	decoding	decoding

What do the different columns mean?

A-This is words per minute. We want to see this number go up. The goal for first grade at the end of the year is 47. B-Errors-This is total mistakes. We want to see this go down. Even just one or two is an improvement. This is also called accuracy. C-Sight words-These are words that don't sound out, like "the." If the number is high, you can practice the sight word lists. D-This is fluency (accuracy, speed, and tone of voice). A 1 is like a robot and a 4 is just like you are talking. E-Chunking-These are missed words that the student should know how to clarify if given time. F-Mispronounced. These mistakes usually involve the student looking at the first letter and guessing. G-Substitutions-These mistakes usually mean that the student guessed what would be next without really looking. H- With these errors, the students were given about three seconds and couldn't make a guess, so they were told the word. I- A mistake that "changes meaning" is a mistake that doesn't really make sense, but the student continues on. J-This is what they remember. A 1 means they didn't remember very much, and a 4 means they remembered at least three good things in a logical order while giving the main idea. K-Hesitations-These are words that the student struggled on but still got right. M-This shows how well they did with decoding multi-syllable words. L-This is how well they decoded. A 1 would mean that they had to sound out most words and a 4 means there were no issues at all. N-This is how many mistakes they made using the short vowel sounds. O-This is how many mistakes they made using the long vowel sounds.

The Overview of Progress Monitoring (Form F) on the following page is used for analyzing all the data on the previous form. It is good for presenting information to the parents. Also, it is useful for planning interventions for the student. This form was described in detail in chapters 13 and 14. You may also make changes to the template at **www.foustreading.simplesite.com.**

Overview of Progress Monitoring

NOTES ON DECODING

How are decoding skills?   Struggling   OK   Does Well

Is there usually a pattern of mistakes?   Yes   No
If so, what?

Do they attempt words they don't know?

Do they usually notice mistakes?

How is sight word recognition?

If extra practice is needed, what do I recommend?

NOTES ON FLUENCY: (Speed, accuracy, and phrasing)

How is fluency?

If fluency is an issue, is their decoding at a high enough level to focus on fluency practice?

What would I recommend for fluency if needed?

NOTES ON COMPREHENSION

How is their retelling?

Does this reflect their use of comprehension skills?

What would I recommend?

APPENDIX 2—Graphic Organizers

In this section, I have included several graphic organizers you can use for enhancing lessons. These organizers will assist in the areas previously discussed. These areas are decoding, fluency, and comprehension. There is a brief description for each one and how it can be used. These graphic organizers can be found at **www.foustreading.simplesite.com**.

Chunk Chart

This chart contains the most common chunks. It also shows the link between the chunks and reading whole words. I use it as a visual to show the students that looking for chunks can help clarify most words.

About 500 easy to read, high frequency words can be derived from these chunks (rimes).

CHUNKING

DECODING

Being effective at "chunking" is almost like a bridge from basic decoding to fluency which could then lead to comprehension.

FLUENCY

ack	ap	ell	in	old	unk
ain	ash	est	ing	op	
ake	at	ice	ink	ore	
ale	ate	ick	ip	ot	
ame	aw	ide	it	uck	
an	ay	ight	ock	ug	
ank	eat	ill	oke	ump	

Clarify Handout

Here is a handout that I use with my students (and their parents) to help them become familiar with "clarifying."

Clarify

1. (if you don't know how to say a word)

Look for chunks and smaller words inside the word.

2. (if you don't know what it means)

Look at the words around it. Look at the pictures. Reread sentence to see if it makes sense.

Decoding Bookmarks

Here are decoding (or clarifying) bookmarks. I will often refer my students to these if they ask me what a word is. We practice these steps every day.

Clarify

Look at the whole word.
"bookcase"

How many syllables?
Count vowels sounds
bookcase=**2 vowel sounds**
2 vowels next to each other
count as one and a sneaky e
doesn't count as a sound

Find each chunk.
bookcase

add letters to each chunk
book+case

Find where to divide.
book/case

Read the word
bookcase

Does it make sense?
If no, try again.

Read the words around it
Does the sentence make sense?

Clarify

Look at the whole word.
"bookcase"

How many syllables?
Count vowels sounds
bookcase=**2 vowel sounds**
2 vowels next to each other
count as one and a sneaky e
doesn't count as a sound

Find each chunk.
bookcase

add letters to each chunk
book+case

Find where to divide.
book/case

Read the word
bookcase

Does it make sense?
If no, try again.

Read the words around it
Does the sentence make sense?

Clarify

Look at the whole word.
"bookcase"

How many syllables?
Count vowels sounds
bookcase=**2 vowel sounds**
2 vowels next to each other
count as one and a sneaky e
doesn't count as a sound

Find each chunk.
bookcase

add letters to each chunk
book+case

Find where to divide.
book/case

Read the word
bookcase

Does it make sense?
If no, try again.

Read the words around it
Does the sentence make sense?

Clarify

Look at the whole word.
"bookcase"

How many syllables?
Count vowels sounds
bookcase=**2 vowel sounds**
2 vowels next to each other
count as one and a sneaky e
doesn't count as a sound

Find each chunk.
bookcase

add letters to each chunk
book+case

Find where to divide.
book/case

Read the word
bookcase

Does it make sense?
If no, try again.

Read the words around it
Does the sentence make sense?

Fluency Scale

Here is a copy of the fluency scale discussed previously. This is a good resource for parents.

Fluency

1. Slow, like a robot. Sounds out words.

2. OK, but still a little slow. May sound out a word or two.

3. Pretty good.

4. Perfect! Sounds like you are talking. Not too fast and not too slow. Reads with expression.

Story Map

This organizer is used to help organize the main parts of a story. These parts are setting, characters, problem, solution, events, and ending. This organizer assists the student in coming up with a good summary.

Story Map

Setting:

Characters: *(who)*

Who is the main character?

Problem:

Why did the problem happen?

Events:
1.
2.
3.
4.
5.
6.
7.
8.
9.
10.

Solution:

Ending:

Summary Hand

This organizer is also used to help organize the main parts of a story. These parts are setting, characters, problem, solution, events, and ending. This organizer assists the student in coming up with a good summary.

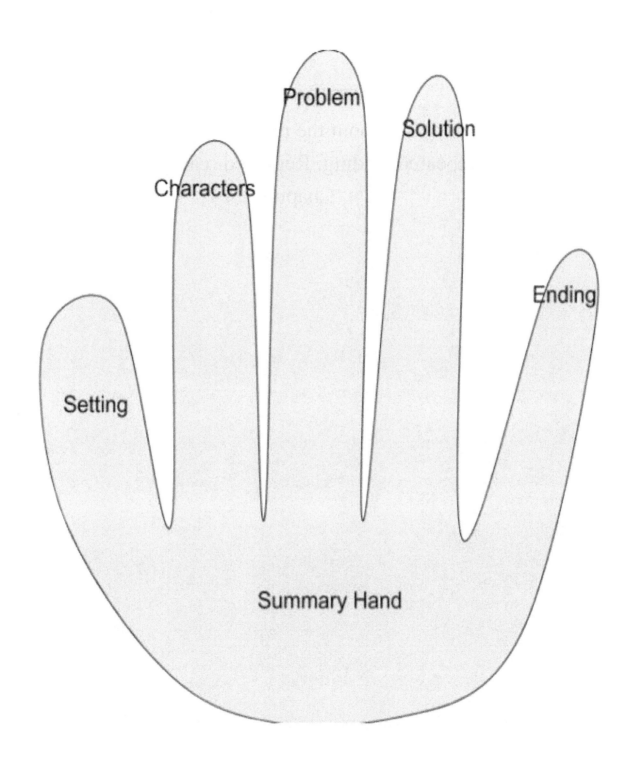

Summary Poem

This is a poem that is about the parts of a good summary. I often use it for repeated reading. Repeated reading is discussed in Chapter 8.

Summary, Summary

Setting, setting, should you care?
You should, you should, it's **when** and **where**.
Is the setting a hot desert at night?
Or is it during the summer at a campsite?

Character, character, it is the **who**.
It could be boy, girl, or animal too.
Look all around, on every page,
You will find the character that is main.

Problem, problem, what goes **wrong**?
Without a problem, a story won't be long.
Would a fairy tale be boring and sad,
If it didn't have a wolf that's bad?

Solution, solution, who **solved** the mess?
Was it someone who wasn't careless?
You see, with a good solution to a story,
Everyone will end up very happy.

Ending, Ending, short and sweet,
A good story **ends** in a way that can't be beat.

Fiction Story Organizer

This organizer is also used to help organize the main parts of a story. These parts are setting, characters, problem, solution, events, and ending. This organizer assists the student in coming up with a good summary.

SETTING

Where does it happen?
When does it happen?
Check every 2 pages to see if it changes.
How does the **setting** affect the story?

PROBLEM

What is the **problem**?
Who caused the **problem**?
Are there any other **problems**?
Who solved the **problem**?
How does the **problem** affect the characters?

ENDING

How did the story end? Did it surprise you? What did you think would happen?

CHARACTERS

Who are the characters?
Who is the **main character**?
Check every 2 pages to see if there are new characters?
How do the characters **change**?

SOLUTION

Who **solved** the problem?
What was done to **solve** the problem?

QUESTIONS

Try to ask questions using these question words after every page

| Who | What |
| Where | When |

PREDICT after every page

Why

5 Ws

I use this as a reminder for the students to ask who, what, when, why, and where questions after every page of a book. I want it to become automatic.

? Who **?**

? What **?**

? Where **?**

? When **?**

? Why **?**

KWL Chart

This organizer is used to help understand non-fiction books. The "K" is what the student already knows about the subject. The "W" is what the student wants to learn about the subject. The "L" is what the student learned after reading the passage.

K	W	L
What I Know	What I Want to Know	What I Learned

Nonfiction Web

This web is used to help ask appropriate questions to aid in the comprehension of nonfiction books or passages.

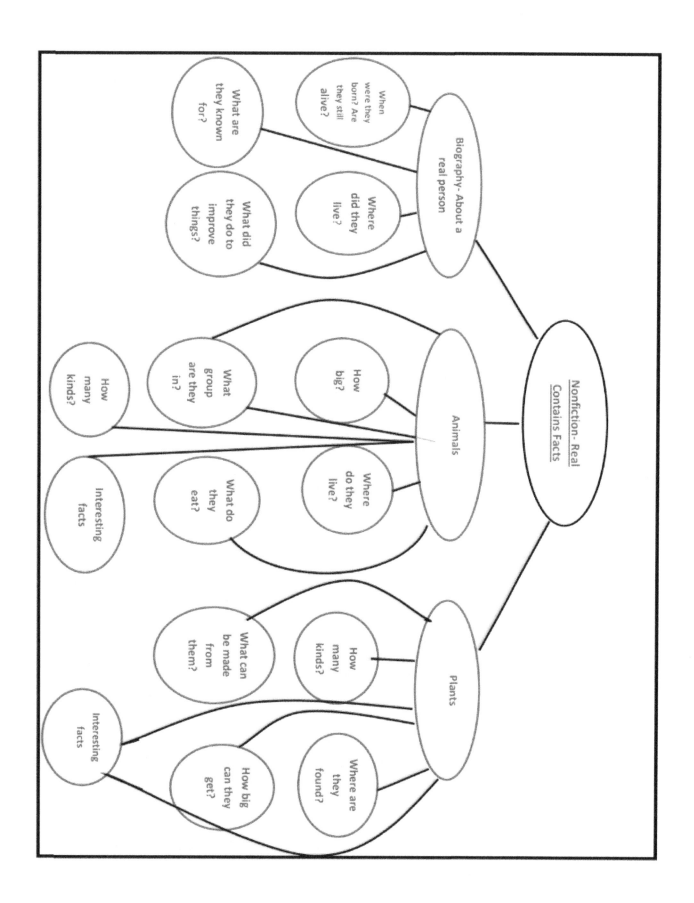

Nonfiction Organizer

This organizer is used to help ask appropriate questions to aid in the comprehension of nonfiction books or passages.

Biography- About a real person

When were they **born**?

Are they still **alive**?

Where did they **live**?

What are they **known** for?

What did they do to **improve** things?

Animals

How **big** can they get?

Where do they **live**?

What **group** do they belong in? (mammals, reptiles, amphibians, birds, fish)

What do they **eat**? (carnivore, herbivore, omnivore)

How many **kinds** are there?

Interesting facts.

Plants

How many **kinds**?

Where are they found?

What can be **made** from them?

How **big** can they get?

Interesting facts?

Places

Where in the world is it?

How many people are in that place?

What is the **weather**?

What is **made** there?

Who is from there?

140

Perfect Practice

This is a handout that I will often review with students. The idea is to have them automatically use these strategies.

Look at the **title**. If it has a picture, look for anything that might be important.

Make a **prediction**. Include a **problem**.

Read carefully. If a word **doesn't sound right**, it probably isn't. Try a different word. Maybe change the <u>vowel sound</u>.

If you don't know what a word means, **read the rest of the sentence**.

Try to read like you are talking (**fluency**).

Be **careful not to skip words**, one little word could change the whole meaning.

On every page, look for **setting, characters, problems, and their possible <u>solutions</u>**.

Think about how the characters **feel** and how their **feelings might change**.

If it is a nonfiction book, look for **facts** on every page.

Made in the USA
Monee, IL
24 August 2021